# INVITATION TO PSALMS

A Short-Term **DISCIPLE** Bible Study

# INVITATION
# TO
# PSALMS

PARTICIPANT BOOK

## Michael Jinkins

*Abingdon Press*
*Nashville*

A Short-Term DISCIPLE Bible Study

INVITATION TO PSALMS
*Copyright © 2008 by Abingdon Press*

This book is printed on recycled, acid-free, elemental chlorine-free paper.

Coin photo by Zev Radovan © Biblical Archaeological Society.

Judith Smith, Interim Editor of Church School Publications;
Mark Price, Senior Editor; Mickey Frith, Associate Editor;
Leo Ferguson, Designer; Marcia C'Debaca, Design Manager

08 09 10 11 12 13 14 15 16 17 — 10 9 8 7 6 5 4 3 2 1
MANUFACTURED IN THE UNITED STATES OF AMERICA

# Contents

# Meet the Writer

MICHAEL JINKINS is an ordained Minister of Word and Sacrament in the Presbyterian Church (USA), having served churches in Irving, Itasca, and Brenham, Texas, and in Aberdeen, Scotland. He serves as Dean of Austin Presbyterian Theological Seminary where he is also Professor of Pastoral Theology. Michael is the author of eleven books, including *In the House of the Lord: Inhabiting the Psalms of Lament* (Liturgical Press, 1998), *The Church Faces Death: Ecclesiology in a Post-Modern Context* (Oxford University Press, 1999), *Invitation to Theology* (InterVarsity Press, 2001), and *Letters to New Pastors* (William B. Eerdmans Publishing Company, 2006).

Besides enjoying poetry and novels, and most recently, sailing, Michael is a huge fan of music, especially blues (B. B. King) and jazz (Miles Davis). He and his wife also enjoy playing golf together as well as following professional golf, sometimes planning their vacations around major PGA events. They look forward to attending their second British Open in the summer of 2008.

# An Invitation
# to This Study

The study you are about to begin is one in a series of short-term, in-depth, small-group Bible studies based on the design of DISCIPLE Bible study. Like the series of long-term DISCIPLE studies, this study has been developed with these underlying assumptions:

- The Bible is the primary text of study.

- Preparation on the part of participants is expected.

- The study leader acts as a facilitator rather than as a lecturer.

- A weekly group session features small-group discussion.

- Video presentations by scholars set the Scriptures in context.

- Encouraging and enhancing Christian discipleship are the goals of the study.

This participant book is your guide to the study and preparation you will do prior to the weekly group meeting. To establish a disciplined pattern of study, first choose a time and a place where you can read, take notes, reflect, and pray. Then choose a good study Bible.

## CHOOSING AND USING
## A STUDY BIBLE

Again, keep in mind that the Bible is *the* text for all short-term DISCIPLE Bible studies, not the participant book; the function of the participant book is to help persons read and listen to the Bible. So because the Bible is the key to this study, consider a couple of recommendations in choosing a good study version of the Bible.

### First: The Translation

The recommended translation is the New Revised Standard Version (NRSV). It is recommended for two reasons: (1) It is a reliable, accurate translation, and (2) it is used in the preparation of all DISCIPLE study manuals.

However, any reliable translation can be used. In fact, having available several different translations is a good practice. Some of them include the NIV, NJB, REB, RSV, NKJV, and NAB. To compare the many English translations of the Bible before choosing, consider consulting the book *The Bible in English Translation: An Essential Guide,* by Steven M. Sheeley and Robert N. Nash, Jr. (Abingdon Press, 1997).

Keep in mind that the *Living Bible* and *The Message,* while popular versions of the Bible, are not considered translations. They are paraphrases.

For this study of Psalms in particular, another recommended study Bible to consider is *The Jewish Study Bible,* TANAKH Translation, published by the Jewish Publication Society (Oxford University Press, 2004). Also, because this study explores Christianity's use of the Psalter in prayer and worship, an additional resource worth having is the Book of Common Prayer, the official service book of the Anglican Communion. The version cited throughout this study is used by the Episcopal Church of the United States of America.

## Second: The Study Features

The recommended Bible to use in any study is, of course, a study Bible—that is, a Bible containing notes, introductions to each book, charts, maps, and other helps designed to deepen and enrich the study of the biblical text. Because there are so many study Bibles available today, be sure to choose one based on some basic criteria:

- The introductory articles to each book or group of books are helpful to you in summarizing the main features of those books.

- The notes illuminate the text of Scripture by defining words, making cross-references to similar passages, and providing cultural or historical background. Keep in mind that the mere volume of notes is not necessarily an indication of their value.

- The maps, charts, and other illustrations display important biblical/historical data in a way that is accurate and accessible.

- Any glossaries, dictionaries, concordances, or indexes in the Bible are easily located and understood.

To a greater or lesser degree, all study Bibles attempt to strike a balance between *interpreting* for the reader what the text means and *helping* the reader understand what the text says. Study Bible notes are conveyed through the interpretive lens of those who prepare the notes. However, regardless of what study Bible you choose to use, always be mindful of which part of the page is Scripture and which part is not.

# GETTING THE MOST FROM READING THE BIBLE

Read the Bible with curiosity. Ask the questions *Who? What? Where? When? How?* and *Why?* as you read.

Learn as much as you can about the passage you are studying. Try to discover what the writer was saying for the time in which the passage was written. Be familiar with the surrounding verses and chapters to establish a passage's setting or situation.

Pay attention to the form of a passage of Scripture. How you read and understand poetry or a parable will differ from how you read and understand a historical narrative.

Above all, let the Scripture speak for itself, even if the apparent meaning is troubling or unclear. Question the Scripture, but also seek answers to your questions in the Scripture itself. Often the biblical text will solve some of the problems that arise in certain passages. Consult additional reference resources when needed. And remember to trust the Holy Spirit to guide you in your study.

# MAKING USE OF ADDITIONAL RESOURCES

Though you will need only the Bible and this participant book to have a meaningful experience, these basic reference books may help you go deeper into your study of Scripture:

- *Eerdmans Dictionary of the Bible*, edited by David Noel Freedman (William B. Eerdmans Publishing Company, 2000).

- *Eerdmans Commentary on the Bible*, edited by James D. G. Dunn and John W. Rogerson (William B. Eerdmans Publishing Company, 2003).

- *The New Interpreter's Bible: A Commentary in Twelve Volumes*, Vol. IV, the commentary on Psalms (Abingdon Press, 1996).

- *Understanding the Old Testament*, fifth edition, by Bernhard W. Anderson, Steven Bishop, and Judith H. Newman (Prentice-Hall, Inc., 2006).

- *The Message of the Psalms: A Theological Commentary*, by Walter Brueggemann (Augsburg Fortress Publishers, 1984).

- *In the House of the Lord: Inhabiting the Psalms of Lament*, by Michael Jinkins (Liturgical Press, 1998).

- *Listening In: A Multicultural Reading of the Psalms*, by Stephen Breck Reid (Abingdon Press, 1997).

- *Answering God: The Psalms as Tools for Prayer*, by Eugene H. Peterson (HarperSanFrancisco, 1989).

- *The Biblical Psalms in Christian Worship: A Brief Introduction and Guide to Resources*, by John D. Witvliet (William B. Eerdmans Publishing Company, 2007).

# MAKING USE OF THE PARTICIPANT BOOK

The participant book serves two purposes. First, it is your study guide: Use it to structure your daily reading of the assigned Scripture passages and to prompt your reflection on what you read. Second, it is your note-taking journal: Use it to write down any insights, comments, and questions you want to recall and perhaps make use of in your group's discussions.

The commentary is full of references to the assigned readings from the Bible and was prepared by a writer who assumed his or her readers would be knowledgeable of the week's Scriptures before coming to the commentary. So the recommended approach to this study is to let the biblical writers have their say first. The hope is that you will see the commentary as one effort to open the biblical text, recognizing that there are almost as many interpretations of Scripture as there are readers.

Throughout the commentary, you will find additional material related to the Psalms printed within a gray background image. That image is in the shape of a silver coin minted during the Bar Kokhba Revolt (132–135 AD). The image depicts a lyre, a musical instrument used in Jewish worship and frequently mentioned in the Psalms.

Following the commentary is an "Invitation to Discipleship" section designed to facilitate reflection on the week's readings as well as a section entitled "For Reflection," which features several questions or reflection exercises and space for your responses. Time to discuss your responses is built into the weekly group meeting.

# Introduction

When I was a child, my family took the occasional summer vacation, usually to the lake or the beach. My most vivid memory, however, was our trip to the Texas Hill Country. We sailed a glass-bottom boat on the San Marcos River and visited the Alamo in San Antonio. Along the way we stopped to see a popular tourist attraction called Wonder Cave. I still remember the words our guide uttered in the haunting depths of this cave created by a shift along the Balcones Fault Line: "You are standing in the middle of an earthquake."

In truth, of course, we were standing in the *result* of an earthquake. But that result was a sight to behold.

Among the most amazing features of our planet are the tectonic plates that grind against one another, pushing up mountain ranges like the Himalayas, cracking open the ocean floor into the Great Rift Valley, and carving out spectacular underground caverns like Wonder Cave. The beauty of these formations is the result of the collisions of massive and powerful landmasses pressing against one another. Similarly, the beauty and power of the Psalms were formed in much the same way: by the result of the collisions of forces, both human and divine, pressing against one another.

In the Psalms, the grand promise of the reign of God meets the historical experience of God's people. The people's faith in God's faithfulness and their trust in God's providential care collide with their ongoing experience of pain and suffering, enslavement, oppression, exile, the consequences of humanity's evil, and the consequences of nature's disregard for life. The struggle of God's people to make sense of who God is and who they are becomes as volatile as the grinding plates of continents. In response to this struggle, the writers of the Psalms praise God for God's faithfulness and lament God's apparent absences. They thank God for God's goodness and complain that God neglects them. They cast their cares upon God in hope and confess terrible dread for the future. And in so doing, they have left behind texts of grace, glory, and sorrow unmatched in sacred literature.

Protestant Reformer John Calvin called the Psalms "An Anatomy of all the Parts of the Soul." Calvin says, "There is not an emotion of which any one can be conscious that is not here represented as in a mirror." The Spirit of God brings to life on these pages "all the griefs, sorrows, fears, doubts, hopes, cares, perplexities, in short, all the distracting emotions" with which our minds are likely to be perplexed. Some parts of the Bible instruct us in God's law; others tell us stories of God's people. The Psalms invite us to pray, reminding us, as Calvin says, that "genuine and earnest prayer proceeds first from a sense of our need, and next, from faith in the promises of God."[1]

Our study is designed to provide three means of access to the Psalms. If we can continue to think along the lines of the guiding metaphor for this study— that of an "earthquake zone"—we will take three different roads into this vast region of tectonic activity where mountains rise and valleys open up to view. So as we go along, let us keep in mind that:

- **The Psalms are prayers** and should be understood as the prayer book of the Bible. We will consider what it means to pray the Psalms, allowing the Psalms—as the Word of God—to give words to our prayers and to speak the Word of God to us in response to our prayers.

- **The Psalms are poetry,** and we will reflect on them as sacred poems, exploring a variety of ways this particular kind of literature communicates certain aspects of the Word of God to us better than any other.

- **The Psalms are expressions of faith.** We will seek to understand better some specific types of psalms and explore more fully how the faith of God's people is reflected in the range of response we find throughout the Book of Psalms.

When we read, hear, and pray the Psalms, we stand within texts torn by earthquakes of the Spirit where God's profound promises meet our own profound needs. This study invites us to engage the Psalms at the deepest levels of our hearts, to plumb the depths of our own experience of God where the tectonic plates of God's faithfulness and our experiences of living collide, compelling us to ask, "How long, O LORD? Will you hide yourself forever?" (Psalm 89:46a), and in the same breath pray, "Great is the LORD and greatly to be praised" (Psalm 48:1a).

# Word of God, Words of Prayer

*But you, O LORD, are a shield around me / my glory, and the one who lifts up my head. / I cry aloud to the LORD, / and he answers me from his holy hill.*

*—Psalm 3:3-4*

## INTRODUCTION

From its opening lines to its closing verse, the Book of Psalms gives expression to a remarkably broad range of praise, thanksgiving, and lamentation. In addition to its variety of voice, the Psalms hold a particularly unique place in the Bible because of their variety of function. First and foremost, the Psalms are prayers, and they are some of the most beautiful poetry ever penned; but the Psalms are also Holy Scripture through which God speaks to us.

Through the Psalms, people of faith have given voice to their highest aspirations, their most common complaints, their deepest regrets, their bitterest accusations against God, their most violent threats against fellow human beings, their most profound confessions of sin, and their most heartfelt adoration of God. The Psalms are human documents tracing the contours of the heart and reflecting the inner face of our humanity, sometimes in the least flattering of lights. But again, the Psalms are also part of the biblical canon. So we begin our encounter with the Book of Psalms by sampling something of the range of prayer offered in them, listening at every turn both for the humanity expressed in these prayers and for the Word of God to us today.

# DAILY ASSIGNMENTS

Many of these psalms from this week's readings are likely to be familiar to you already. Take your time reading them, allowing the words of each psalm to soak into your soul and become your own prayer to God.

## DAY ONE: Psalms 1; 2

These psalms stand like a grand entrance to the entire Book of Psalms. Psalms 1 and 2 establish the seismic tensions running throughout the whole collection by stating the expectation that those who love God will ultimately prosper. Listen for how the psalms articulate this expectation and then immediately call it into question in light of human experience.

## DAY TWO: Psalms 3–7

The tension anticipated in Psalms 1 and 2 surfaces explicitly in these powerful psalms and resurfaces repeatedly throughout the Book of Psalms, especially in the psalms of lament. Listen for the frankness of the anxieties and complaints of the psalmist, as well as for the underlying trust the psalmist continues to place in God.

## DAY THREE: Psalms 13; 22

Notice how, in a short span of verses, Psalm 13 takes us from the depths of lamentation, "How long, O LORD? Will you forget me forever?" (13:1), to the pinnacle of praise, "I will sing to the LORD, / because he has dealt bountifully with me" (13:6). Psalm 22 remains for Christians the most familiar and theologically important of all the psalms of lament, often described as the psalm of the Crucifixion or the Passion of Christ. As you read it, reflect especially on the opening line, knowing that Christ spoke these words from the cross. How does this affect their meaning?

## DAY FOUR: Psalm 23

Psalms that express our trust in the Lord abound. Some have become so familiar to us that we take for granted their originality, power, and depth. Read Psalm 23 in the New Revised Standard Version (NSRV), the King James Version (KJV), and in another translation of your choice. What surprises you about the portrait of God painted here? Now, reread Psalm 22 and go on directly into Psalm 23 again. Why do you think those who assembled the Book of Psalms placed these psalms next to one another?

## DAY FIVE: Psalm 51

Psalm 51 is a penitential psalm, traditionally seen as the response to some of the bleakest and most desperate days in the life of King David. Read Psalm 51, and then read 2 Samuel 11–12 to hear the story the editors of the Psalms used to connect this psalm to the life of David. What was the nature of David's sin? What was the role of the prophet in relation to the king? What was David's response to Nathan's words? Now pray Psalm 51 as your own prayer. How do you sense seeds of confession taking root in your own heart? How do you resist this prayer? How do you respond to it?

## DAY SIX:

Read the commentary in the participant book.

# PRAYED SCRIPTURE

Dietrich Bonhoeffer, the German minister executed by the Nazis near the end of World War II, referred to the Psalms as the "prayerbook of the Bible."[1] He insisted that the Psalms be understood in the context of the whole Bible, that they be heard in conversation with the entire canon of Christian Scripture.

Bonhoeffer's approach was not intended to limit the Psalms or to alienate them from their roots in Judaism, but rather to locate Christians in a larger tradition of faith. His approach had the effect both of recovering the Old Testament as a Christian witness to Jesus Christ and of recognizing the covenantal relatedness of Christians to those who worship the God of Abraham, Isaac, and Jacob. By doing this, Bonhoeffer rejected the superficial piety of those who cut off Christianity from the life-giving streams of Old Testament traditions, the Torah, the Prophets, and the Writings. He also countered the spiritual and political exclusivity of those who believed that faith in Christ gave them a monopoly on God. All of these issues were of critical importance in Bonhoeffer's world, and they continue to be important to this day.

As Bonhoeffer reminds us, the humanity of the Psalms does not detract from the fact that they speak God's Word: "At first it is something very astonishing that there is a prayerbook in the Bible. The Holy Scriptures are, to be sure, God's Word to us. But prayers are human words. How then do they come to be in the Bible? Let us make no mistake: the Bible is God's Word, even in the Psalms."[2] These human prayers, often movingly human and sometimes shockingly inhumane utterances spoken under all sorts of conditions, also speak for God as we hear them in the larger context of the gospel of Jesus Christ. The Word of God never exists hermetically sealed in isolation from human history.

## Luther on the Psalms

"The Psalter ought to be a dear and beloved book, if only because it promises Christ's death and resurrection so clearly, and so typifies His kingdom and the condition and nature of all Christendom that it might well be called a little Bible."[3]

*(Martin Luther)*

The whole of the Christian canon reflects God's enduring covenant of grace with God's creation.

In his commentary on the Psalms, scholar J. Clinton McCann argues that while the Psalms must be interpreted "both as humanity's words to God and as God's word to humanity," the same is in fact true for every other part of the Bible. "*All* Scripture originated as the record of humanity's encounter with and response to God, a record that generations of God's people judged to be authentic and true; thus it was preserved and transmitted as the Word of God."[4]

Our study seeks to understand the Psalms in much the same spirit in which Bonhoeffer, McCann, and others understand them, viewing the Psalms and the Bible from an "incarnational" perspective. The Bible bears witness to the God who became flesh. The Bible never stops being a product of human efforts even as it becomes the instrument through which God speaks to us. Our reading of the Bible as a whole, in light of Jesus Christ, reflects God's own dealings with the world.

### Psalms in the New Testament

"By one count there are 196 citations of the Psalms in the New Testament, counting parallels in the Gospels as individual items.... These citations are of thirty-five psalms. Functionally, then, the Psalms are treated as Scripture, whatever their precise canonical status was in the various circles of the first-century church."[5]

*(William L. Holladay)*

However, this is not all it means to understand the Psalms as the prayer book of the Bible. Reading, hearing, *and praying* the Psalms from within the context of the Old and New Testaments also means that, as Christians, we pray the Psalms *through Jesus Christ.*

## IN THE NAME OF JESUS

Our faith as disciples of Jesus of Nazareth is given voice by the Psalms. Our faith as followers of Jesus is also brought into even deeper conflict because of the Psalms. The Psalms force us to reexamine all aspects of our lives, including areas we seldom wish to recognize. For instance, the Psalms compel us to examine theologically the desire we sometimes feel for our enemies to get what's coming to them, or our sense that life should always work out comfortably and profitably for those who love God. The Psalms call us to bring all aspects of human life consciously into the presence of God in prayer.

It is not uncommon for Christians who are just beginning to pray the whole Book of Psalms to feel uncomfortable praying certain psalms. Some of the psalms call upon God to inflict suffering and even death on those who oppose us. Others reflect a disturbing self-righteousness on the part of the writers. Some psalms reflect the writers' belief that their ways are God's ways and that those who oppose them inevitably oppose God and therefore should be punished. Such psalms are not easy to pray as a Christian. Several years ago, a friend said to me of his own practice of praying the Psalms, "You know, there are some prayers I simply have to trust Jesus Christ to pray *for* me."

As we pray the Psalms, we offer them up as our own words, human words forged in the crucible of painful experience and transformation, words preserved for generations of the faithful. In so doing, all parts of human life (for there is nothing from the depths to the heights of human experience that is not preserved in the Psalms) are brought to God in prayer. Our adoration and thanksgiving are offered as sacrifices of praise to God. Our complaints and petitions are placed in God's hands. Our hope for justice and our desire for revenge are left at God's feet in the awareness that judgment and vindication belong to God alone. Through Christ, we can pray every prayer in the confidence of children, knowing that God will see through our prayers to the heart that holds nothing back from God.

The Psalms draw us to give thanks for things we often take for granted. They can ignite in our hearts raptures of praise and adoration for an infinitely adorable God and wonder at the greatness of God's creative power and mercy. They can also force from the shadows of unconsciousness our lust for vengeance, making us bear even this into the light of God's grace. They demand that we leave our yearnings for justice to God as well as the fate of those who have harmed us.

The Psalms serve as the ultimate spiritual catharsis for the revenge-ravaged soul and the ultimate antidote to the spiritual denial that afflicts us. When the Psalms make our hearts soar, and even when they make us wince (and sometimes they do!), it is hard not to recognize our voices emerging from their words. When we hear ourselves praying aloud what we have been unable to confess even to ourselves, we are often able to say at long last, "Lord, forgive *me*, the sinner."

The Psalms teach us to pray by teaching us to entrust all of life to God, recognizing there is no part of our lives that does not belong to God. "Thus," Bonhoeffer writes, "it does not matter whether the Psalms express exactly what we feel in our heart at the moment we pray. Perhaps it is precisely the case that we must pray against our own heart in order to pray rightly. It is not just that for which we ourselves want to pray that is important, but that for which God wants us to pray."[6]

# INVITATION TO DISCIPLESHIP

The psalmist reminds us that all of life belongs to God. Entering the Psalms, we encounter a realm of peace and wholeness that we identify with the reign of God. We cannot read these psalms without risking a deeper involvement in the life of faith; and we cannot pray them without risking the loss of our hearts to God's reign.

As we continue to study the Psalms in the days to come, we will undoubtedly find ourselves troubled as much as comforted by their message. At times we will find healing, grace, and encouragement. But at other times, we will hear a message of justice and righteousness that pricks our conscience, a clarion call to trust in God above all else, and an urgent plea to obey God's law.

The Psalms reach across the ages, take us by the lapels, shake us from our complacencies, and remind us that the ways of the wicked are like chaff blown away by the wind (Psalm 1) and the forces of the most powerful nations are laughably impotent in comparison with the Lord (Psalm 2).

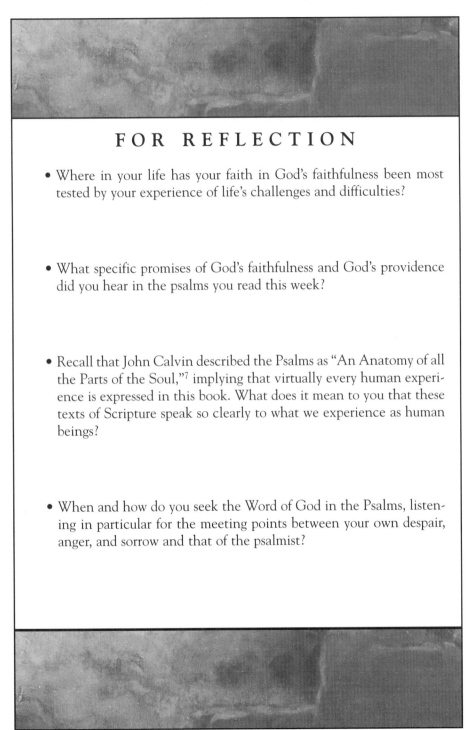

# FOR REFLECTION

- Where in your life has your faith in God's faithfulness been most tested by your experience of life's challenges and difficulties?

- What specific promises of God's faithfulness and God's providence did you hear in the psalms you read this week?

- Recall that John Calvin described the Psalms as "An Anatomy of all the Parts of the Soul,"[7] implying that virtually every human experience is expressed in this book. What does it mean to you that these texts of Scripture speak so clearly to what we experience as human beings?

- When and how do you seek the Word of God in the Psalms, listening in particular for the meeting points between your own despair, anger, and sorrow and that of the psalmist?

# Five Books in One

The Book of Psalms is arranged into five sections, called books. Scholars contend this editorial arrangement parallels the five-book division of the Torah (Genesis through Deuteronomy). Each of the five sections of psalms ends with a doxology, a short praise that begins, "Blessed be the LORD" or "Praise the LORD."

Book I: Psalms 1–41 (doxology: Psalm 41:13)

Book II: Psalms 42–72 (doxology: Psalm 72:18-19)

Book III: Psalms 73–89 (doxology: Psalm 89:52)

Book IV: Psalms 90–106 (doxology: Psalm 106:48)

Book V: Psalms 107–150
(doxology: Psalm 150)

# The Prayer Book of God's People

*Blessed be the name of the* LORD */ from this time on and forevermore. / From the rising of the sun to its setting / the name of the* LORD *is to be praised.*

—*Psalm 113:2-3*

## INTRODUCTION

The Psalms as we have them today are a collection of prayers, hymns, and sacred poems expressing the faith of the people of Israel. For centuries they have been used in public worship, in family devotions, and in private prayer. The title of the collection in the Hebrew Scripture is *Tehillim*. This means simply the Praises, or the Book of Praises. Our word *Psalms* is drawn from the Greek translation of this title, *Psalmoi*. The Psalms themselves reflect a variety of uses in the worship of the Jewish people over the centuries. Indeed, many of the ancient uses of the Psalms in worship are indelibly stamped on the Psalms themselves.

The Psalms were used for prayer and singing not only in the temples and synagogues of Judaism, but also in worshiping congregations in the earliest expressions of the Christian church as it emerged as a movement from within Judaism. While we ordinarily think of the Psalms as a discrete book in the Old Testament, there are, in fact, psalms scattered throughout the whole Bible, including the New Testament. As we will see in our readings this week, Mary's song, also known as the *Magnificat* (Luke 1:46-55) and Simeon's Song, the *Nunc Dimittis* (Luke 2:29-32), are examples of New Testament psalms. Our study will explore the uses of the Psalms as the prayer book of the people of God, including their uses in ancient Judaism.

# DAILY ASSIGNMENTS

This week we will begin by looking at several psalms located outside the Book of Psalms in order to gain a deeper sense of the relationship of psalms to the life and liturgy of God's people. Those readings assigned from the Book of Psalms will relate thematically to the other texts.

Before proceeding, it may be helpful to define the word *liturgy*. It comes from the Greek word *leiturgia* and refers literally to the work of the people. Today, liturgy commonly signifies the specific work that the people of God do in worship. But this work is closely connected with all the other kinds of work the people do, reminding us of Paul's admonition to worship and serve God in Romans 12:1-2. We live our lives of faith in thankful obedience. We praise God in light of all that occurs in our daily lives.

### DAY ONE: Exodus 15; Psalm 136

The Exodus passage includes two biblical psalms: the Song of Moses (15:1-18) and the Song of Miriam (15:20-21). Both psalms portray the people of Israel as responding in praise and thanksgiving to their deliverance from slavery in Egypt, as though to say, "Whenever God acts, the appropriate human response is praise!" The Song of Moses not only remembers what God has accomplished, it also anticipates what God will yet do, explicitly connecting God's faithfulness in the past to God's promises for the future.

Consider Exodus 15 in light of this question: When you know God has acted in your life, how do you usually respond?

## DAY TWO: 1 Samuel 2:1-10; Psalm 113

Like the songs of Moses and Miriam, Hannah's prayer leaps out at the reader from the story in which it is embedded. Moses and Miriam respond to the deliverance of Israel from bondage. God's deliverance, to which Hannah responds, is of a much more intimate sort.

Read the first chapter of 1 Samuel (which provides the context of the story) and 2:1-10 (the psalm of praise). What do the two psalms in Exodus 15 and the one in 1 Samuel 2 have in common? How are they different?

## DAY THREE: Lamentations 5; Psalm 44

The Book of Lamentations consists entirely of psalms of lament written after the destruction of Jerusalem by the Babylonians in 586/7 BC. The grief expressed in these psalms is heartbreaking and unrelenting. The people own their guilt and repent in humility, praying for redemption. After reading Lamentations 5, reflect on this question: What is the significance of the fact that Christians have traditionally used readings from Lamentations during Holy Week?

## DAY FOUR: Luke 1:46-55; 2:29-32; Psalm 96

Nowhere are the Jewish roots of Christianity more evident than in the continuity between Old and New Testament psalms. In the Song of Mary (the *Magnificat*) and the Song of Simeon (*Nunc Dimittis*), the great themes of the praise of Israel unite with the gospel of Jesus Christ as the name of the Lord is magnified and the reign of God on earth is proclaimed. Consider how these songs compare to the psalms from the Old Testament.

## DAY FIVE: Matthew 6:1-18; Psalm 24

There is no more appropriate place for our reading of psalms outside the Book of Psalms to culminate than in the Lord's Prayer. Jesus provides his followers with both instruction on how to pray and with a model prayer.

After reading Matthew 6:1-18, go back to verses 9-13 and pray the Lord's Prayer. Then reflect on this question: What warnings and promises does the Lord's Prayer hold for those shaken by life's rending forces?

## DAY SIX:

Read the commentary in the participant book.

# THE BOOK OF PRAISES

The Bible reflects something so obvious about the nature of prayer that we sometimes miss it: God's acts inevitably evoke a human response.

Eugene Peterson describes the Psalms as "acts of obedience, answering the God who has addressed us." This is what it means to say that the Psalms are prayers, because prayer is always a response to God. Peterson continues:

> God's word precedes these words: these prayers don't seek God, they respond to the God who seeks us.... God comes and speaks—his word catches us in sin, finds us in despair, invades us by grace. The Psalms are our answers. We don't always like what God speaks to us, and we don't always understand it. Left to ourselves, we will pray to some god who speaks what we like hearing, or to the part of God that we manage to understand. But what is critical is that we speak to the God who speaks to us, and to everything that he speaks to us, and in our speaking ... mature in the great art of conversation with God that is prayer.[1]

The Psalms as prayers respond to the Word who is God, and in their response the Psalms become the Word of God to us. Praying the Psalms draws us into this profound and rich conversation. This speech and response goes to the very heart of the divine-human encounter.

In psalms, we voice the most basic, elemental aspects of our faith. We give thanksgiving and praise in psalms like the Song of Moses, and we utter our cries of desolation and grief as recorded in the Book of Lamentations. We express our sense of gratitude at the presence of God, our terror at God's apparent absence, and our pleas for God to grant something we desperately need.

## The Genius of the Psalms

"This is the particular genius of the psalms: they instruct our feelings without negating them. They draw upon our particular experience of God as at the same time they expand it exponentially."[2]

*(Ellen F. Davis)*

The Psalms take seriously the full range of human experience. They do not hold it against us that we pray to God in tight spots. According to the Psalms, foxhole faith is not necessarily shallow faith, if in fact it encourages us to dig deeper.

Note that a psalm soaring with the rhetoric of devotion—"As a deer longs for flowing streams, / so my soul longs for you, O God"—is the very same psalm that reveals a person tossing and turning and pacing the hours away in anxiety: "My tears have been my food / day and night, / while people say to me continually, / 'Where is your God?'" (Psalm 42:1, 3) The honesty of the Psalms invites us to be candid before God.

The Psalms also invite us to allow the responses of the psalmists to become our own. But keep this in mind: The often spare lines of verse in the Psalms—the direct, sometimes ascetic expressions of praise, trust, and lament—invite us into the deepest places of our faith. Indeed, the theology of the Psalms runs counter to the comfortable, popular piety of today that implies if we "pray" the right formula, God will give us whatever we ask. Such piety finds no home in the Psalms.

The God to whom the psalmist pours out his heart is the living God, the holy God, the free and just Creator of all that exists, the sovereign ruler of all nations. We offer our lives to this God; we do not use this God for our own ends.

The Psalms reconnect us with a language that means fully and precisely what it says. Unsentimental and unpretentious, the Psalms refuse to avert the eyes of faith from even the most disturbing aspects of life. Everyone—even God—is held accountable in the Psalms, and in no uncertain terms. When laments are offered by the psalmists, only lamentation will do. When curses are expressed, it is because wrath is due. When thanks are given, gratitude is intended, not groveling. When praise is offered, it is because nothing less than the praise of God is appropriate. So we learn the rhythms of a life lived faithfully in the school of the Psalms, praying what needs to be prayed in response to the Word of God.

# A BOOK OF WORSHIP FOR ALL

As we saw in the readings this week, psalms occur throughout the Bible and are related to particular events, whether vast, history-altering events like the destruction of Jerusalem and the exile of God's people, or events on the most intimate level between a mother, a father, and a child. Turning to the Book of Psalms, we find within this single collection the astonishing variety of prayer responses to the God of Israel.

While particular psalms were often written in response to a specific event (or at least connected by the editors of the Psalms to an event recorded in sacred texts), the collection we know as the Book of Psalms is designed as a kind of combination hymnal, prayer book, and book of corporate worship. The Book of Psalms was clearly used for public purposes. It also contains elements of a private or family devotional. By any standards, the Book of Psalms is both a very *personal* and *public* text. Like the hymnals that many of us use in our congregations today, the Book of Psalms incorporates some texts of great antiquity and others of much more recent vintage.

Many scholars believe that entire sections of the Book of Psalms were collected for use in worship as early as the reign of King David, the second king of Israel (1000–962 BC). The collection of the Psalms, essentially as we have it today, was certainly used as the prayer book of the Second Temple—that is, the Temple built *after* the people of Israel returned from exile. The Second Temple was completed in Jerusalem in 515 BC, replacing Solomon's Temple, which was destroyed by the Babylonians in 586/7 BC. But within the Book of Psalms, there are collections of psalms that may have been used as a liturgical resource much earlier.

## Superscriptions

The superscriptions are editorial comments that appear under the psalm number and before the first line of the psalm itself. Some superscriptions give instructions for how a psalm is to be used in worship. For example: "To the leader: with stringed instruments. A Psalm. A Song" (Psalm 67). Some superscriptions refer to musical terms or musical instruments that had already disappeared from usage when the Psalms were translated from Hebrew into Greek. For example: "To the leader: according to The Gittith. Of Asaph" (Psalm 81). Other superscriptions identify the author of the psalm text. Of the more than one hundred superscriptions in the Book of Psalms, seventy-three refer to David.

The Book of Psalms we hold in our hands today is something like an archae-ological site, like a city built upon past cities. One layer of text stands upon another like layers of houses and streets pancaked upon each other, but with this important difference: The layers of texts are often rather jumbled up, not unlike our modern hymnals and books of worship. Some psalms, the core of which date from King David himself, stand beside or near psalms from other ages. There is a psalm "of Solomon" (Psalm 127) sitting next to a psalm that refers directly to the experience of the exiled people of Israel (Psalm 126), with another exilic psalm (Psalm 137) only a stone's throw away. One entire col-lection of psalms (Psalms 3–41), within the larger Book of Psalms, is almost entirely ascribed to King David.

Certain psalms refer to God as *Yahweh*, the sacred name of Israel's God ren-dered as "the LORD," while other psalms favor *Elohim*, the word for "God" in Hebrew. Some psalms may have been designed from the very beginning to be set to music. Others appear to have been used by pilgrims as chants in spe-cific liturgical acts at the Temple. Still others may have been employed pri-marily in family gatherings (for example, in observance of Passover) rather than in the Temple.[3]

The Book of Psalms has been used for centuries. The praying of the Psalms in Jewish synagogues echoed in the early house churches and the first simple basilicas of the Christian movement. The chanting of the Psalms in the monasteries and cathedrals of medieval Europe lives on in new forms in con-gregations around the world. The Genevan and the Scottish Psalters, both of which were products of the sixteenth-century Protestant Reformation, estab-lished the singing of the Psalms as an integral part of Christian worship.[4] The hymns of Isaac Watts and Charles Wesley often created new "psalms" theologically echoing those contained in the Book of Psalms, but centered on the gospel of Jesus Christ. The biblical psalms inspired and provided the fundamental forms of praise used in the development of Christian hymnody. Today we find the Psalms emerging in the lyrical repetitions of praise songs and in beautiful chant-response settings for psalms composed by con-temporary hymnists.

# INVITATION TO DISCIPLESHIP

As a child, I took for granted how difficult and important it was to see adults such as my grandparents or my pastor bow their heads and hear them pray out loud. This practice of praying in an improvised fashion rather than from a pre-pared text is one of the most demanding and valuable practices of faith. Yet it is so easy for these prayers to become little more than trite exercises that fail to express the richness and fullness of personal faith. This is where the Psalms can help.

The Psalms invite readers into the practice of giving voice to our faith out of the deep wells of ancient faith expressed within the Bible. Whether we pray aloud in worship or around a table at mealtime, whether we bless a child about to be married or lament the loss of a loved one, we would do well to learn the language of the psalmists.

To that end, consider this method of letting the Psalms guide your praying for next few days: Each day, spend a few minutes writing by hand the words of one of the Psalms. Try incorporating this discipline even into your daily prayers. Pay attention to how, over time, the words of the psalmists enter into your own extemporaneous prayers and give them new depth and power—a benefit to you as well as to others.

## The Genevan Psalter

Believing that worship should include the singing of the Psalms, Reformation theologian John Calvin enlisted the help of Clément Marot, court poet of France, and Theodorus Beza to set all 150 psalms in metrical French. The resulting Genevan Psalter was published in 1562. Congregations sang the Psalms without accompaniment since Calvin also believed instrumental music to be distracting to the worshiper. Owing largely to the Genevan Psalter, psalm singing became a defining characteristic of Reformed worship in the sixteenth and seventeenth centuries.

# FOR REFLECTION

- The Psalms are dedicated to the worship of one God in contrast to false gods. In what ways do the Psalms curb our tendency to create a god in our own image who speaks only what we want to hear?

- Contrast the character of the God who cannot be manipulated with the false gods who promise to provide what we want if we perform the "right" rituals.

- What is the significance of the idea that the God of the Psalms is sovereign over all nations and peoples and cannot be contained in any single creed (even our own)?

- Where do you see evidence that the Psalms are stretching your own understanding of God?

# Praying the Psalms

*To you, O LORD, I lift up my soul. / O my God, in you I trust.*

*—Psalm 25:1*

## INTRODUCTION

The Psalms are essentially prayers. Much can be learned about the Psalms by studying them in a variety of ways—as poetry, blessings, confessional statements, and liturgical artifacts illuminating the ancient worship of Israel. But to understand the Psalms on their own terms, we must pray them.

Obviously there are many ways to pray the Psalms. Psalms are often used as public prayers to call the congregation to worship: "Praise the LORD! / O give thanks to the LORD, for he is good; / for his steadfast love endures forever" (Psalm 106:1). "Bless the LORD, O my soul, / and all that is within me, / bless his holy name. / Bless the LORD, O my soul, / and do not forget all his benefits" (Psalm 103:1-2). Congregations use the Psalms as part of the Common Lectionary to respond to the Old

Testament reading on the Lord's Day. Congregations also use the Psalms to express their hopes and to give voice to their concerns in litanies, hymns, and songs of praise. The practice of singing and chanting the Psalms in worship has undergone a contemporary renaissance. Psalms are now being arranged for musical settings that respect and reflect their texts even better than the metrical psalms we inherited from the Scottish and Genevan Psalters. Psalms are also often used in family and individual devotions on special occasions, at times of particular trial or celebration, or as a part of a regular, daily discipline. All of these contemporary uses of the Psalms have their roots in both Judaism and Christianity.

# DAILY ASSIGNMENTS

This week we will simply pray the Psalms. The practice of praying the Psalms on a regular schedule *ad seriatim*—that is, one psalm following another, day after day, through the whole Psalter over the course of the month, year in and year out—has been around since the beginning of the church. This session of our study will introduce this simple practice and explore the wisdom of learning the Psalms from the inside out, allowing them to enter our vocabulary of devotion steadily and inviting them to become a living resource to our faith.

There are many resources that provide a daily selection of the Psalms for prayer and meditation. One of the best and most straightforward is the division of the Psalms for daily prayer found in the Book of Common Prayer. Treasured for centuries in the Anglican tradition, this resource organizes the praying of a few psalms each morning and evening to complete a reading of all the Psalms each month. This morning and evening practice produces a natural rhythm in one's life, framing the day in praise of God.

For the next five days, we will pray a set of psalms as arranged by the Book of Common Prayer. The full month's schedule is printed on the following pages. Keep in mind that you will only follow the schedule for five days, beginning with the day of the month corresponding to the day you start your daily reading assignment. For instance, if the day you plan to start reading is the tenth day of the month, locate Day 10 and read the psalm(s) designated for morning prayer and those designated for evening prayer. Follow the same pattern for Days 11 through 14 to complete five days of readings. On the sixth day of this week, as usual, read the commentary in the participant book.

## SCHEDULE FOR PRAYING THE PSALMS MONTHLY

**Day 1**      *Morning*—Psalms 1–5   ◆   *Evening*—Psalms 6–8

**Day 2**      *Morning*—Psalms 9–11   ◆   *Evening*—Psalms 12–14

**Day 3**      *Morning*—Psalms 15–17   ◆   *Evening*—Psalm 18

**Day 4**      *Morning*—Psalms 19–21   ◆   *Evening*—Psalms 22–23

**Day 5**      *Morning*—Psalms 24–26   ◆   *Evening*—Psalms 27–29

**Day 6**      *Morning*—Psalms 30–31   ◆   *Evening*—Psalms 32–34

**Day 7**      *Morning*—Psalms 35–36   ◆   *Evening*—Psalm 37

**Day 8**      *Morning*—Psalms 38–40   ◆   *Evening*—Psalms 41–43

**Day 9**      *Morning*—Psalms 44–46   ◆   *Evening*—Psalms 47–49

**Day 10**      *Morning*—Psalms 50–52   ◆   *Evening*—Psalms 53–55

**Day 11**      *Morning*—Psalms 56–58   ◆   *Evening*—Psalms 59–61

**Day 12**      *Morning*—Psalm 62–64   ◆   *Evening*—Psalms 65–67

**Day 13**      *Morning*—Psalm 68   ◆   *Evening*—Psalms 69–70

**Day 14**      *Morning*—Psalms 71–72   ◆   *Evening*—Psalms 73–74

**Day 15**      *Morning*—Psalms 75–77   ◆   *Evening*—Psalm 78

**Day 16**     *Morning*—Psalms 79–81   ◆   *Evening*—Psalms 82–85

**Day 17**     *Morning*—Psalms 86–88   ◆   *Evening*—Psalm 89

**Day 18**     *Morning*—Psalms 90–92   ◆   *Evening*—Psalms 93–94

**Day 19**     *Morning*—Psalms 95–97   ◆   *Evening*—Psalms 98–101

**Day 20**     *Morning*—Psalms 102–103   ◆   *Evening*—Psalm 104

**Day 21**     *Morning*—Psalm 105   ◆   *Evening*—Psalm 106

**Day 22**     *Morning*—Psalm 107   ◆   *Evening*—Psalms 108–109

**Day 23**     *Morning*—Psalms 110–113   ◆   *Evening*—Psalms 114–115

**Day 24**     *Morning*—Psalms 116–118   ◆   *Evening*—Psalm 119:1-32

**Day 25**     *Morning*—Psalm 119:33-72   ◆   *Evening*—Psalm 119:73-104

**Day 26**     *Morning*—Psalm 119:105-144   ◆   *Evening*—Psalm 119:145-176

**Day 27**     *Morning*—Psalms 120–125   ◆   *Evening*—Psalms 126–131

**Day 28**     *Morning*—Psalms 132–135   ◆   *Evening*—Psalms 136–138

**Day 29**     *Morning*—Psalms 139–140   ◆   *Evening*—Psalms 141–143

**Day 30**     *Morning*—Psalms 144–146   ◆   *Evening*—Psalms 147–150

# NOTES

### Day One Readings

| Morning | ◆ | Evening |
|---|---|---|
| | | |

### Day Two Readings

| Morning | ◆ | Evening |
|---|---|---|
| | | |

### Day Three Readings

| Morning | ◆ | Evening |
|---|---|---|
| | | |

## Day Four Readings

| Morning 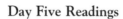 | Evening |
|---|---|
| | |

## Day Five Readings

| Morning | Evening |
|---|---|
| | |

## Day Six Reading (Commentary)

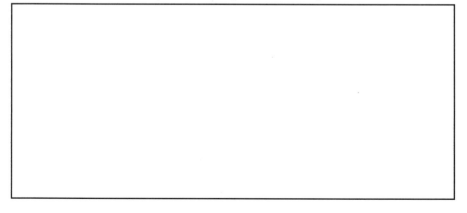

# A PRACTICE OF FAITH

Several years ago, I began a prayer group for students and staff at my seminary. The group, which varies in membership somewhat each semester, enters into a covenant to pray the Psalms daily using the Book of Common Prayer and to read each day an assigned portion of a classic of Christian spirituality—something written by Julian of Norwich, Thomas Merton, Henri J. M. Nouwen, or someone similar.

At the beginning of each semester, mindful of the new members of the group, I ask participants to refrain from discussing the Psalms in our weekly meetings until we have prayed all the way through all 150 psalms at least once. When at last I invite the group to reflect on their experience of praying the Psalms, the conversation is like opening a floodgate: Ideas, joys, concerns, frustrations, questions, and experiences of serendipity and shock all tumble over one another to be expressed.

One student might say, "I came in from class tired and worried one night last week. I had started to think I don't belong in this community, that maybe I don't belong in seminary, that maybe God has no use for me in the church. Frankly I didn't feel like praying the Psalms that night, but I promised the group I would, so I did. And that night as I prayed the Psalms, I heard exactly what I needed to hear. I was comforted at the deepest level of my being. I was reminded that I belong, no matter how I feel. I do belong."

The Psalms can provide comfort and hope and promise in times when we most need a word of holy encouragement.

Another participant might counter, "I have never had such a jarring experience in my life as praying the Psalms. I kept thinking to myself that someone should put a muzzle on the psalmist. I expect Scripture to uplift and inspire. But these psalms just bother me! They disturb and unsettle me! They raise all sorts of questions!" And off the student goes with questions and concerns the Psalms have provoked. Thus, the Psalms sometimes can act like a pebble in the previously comfortable shoes of faith.

After leading these covenant groups over the years in congregations and now on a seminary campus, I have come to believe that praying the Psalms daily is among the most valuable and powerful practices of the faith in the history of the church.

# HABITS WORTH HAVING

Habits often get a bad rap in our culture. Sometimes the only habits we think about are the bad ones we are trying to break. However, sometimes we do not think much of good habits either. We suspect perhaps that habits are nothing more than flying on moral automatic pilot. The ideals of sincerity and authenticity that have dominated much modern religious thinking since the nineteenth century imply that habits are not *sincere* or *authentic* moral behavior. They lack spontaneity and are not adequately feeling-oriented.

In the classical world of Aristotle, people tended to hold precisely the opposite view. In Latin, for instance, the word for "habit" means at its root "having" and "holding." According to this understanding, a person's character is the way one *holds* one's self in relation to others. The ancients believed that in the formation of a person's character, *having* and *holding* one's self requires the cultivation of virtuous habits. And the cultivation of virtuous habits takes discipline and careful attention over time. According to the classical thinkers, we are the sum of the habits we regularly practice.

My grandmother was an especially adept practitioner of classical moral philosophy—though she did not know it. She had never read Aristotle, but she knew her Bible and she prayed her Psalter. I remember as a child that whenever I did something naughty, she would say to me something like, "I should think you'd respect yourself too much to do that kind of thing, young man. I certainly hope you don't make a habit of that." She expected me to form a set of appropriate habits that would be in force in my life no matter what I felt like doing at a particular moment. In her view,

## Psalms and St. Benedict's Rule

"The words of the psalm are: I have uttered your praises seven times during the day [Psalm 119:164]. We shall fulfill that sacred number of seven if at the times of Lauds, Prime, Terce, Sext, None, Vespers and Compline we perform the duty of our service to God.... About the night Vigil that same psalm says: In the middle of the night I arose to praise you [Psalm 119:62]. And so at these times let us offer praise to our Creator."[1]

*(St. Benedict)*

the habit of telling the truth should trump my desire to get out of a scrape by lying and blaming someone else for what I had done. The habit of honesty should prevent me from stealing the quarter in someone else's school desk even if I had an urge to eat a candy bar at recess. According to Aristotle and my grandmother, the habits we develop are an outward expression of who we are. It is simply impossible to win an argument about your character if your habits are arguing against you.

Habits have the power to shape character. But habits also have the power to form beliefs.

Some years ago, as I was going through a struggle in my faith, a friend told me a story. He said that while he served as a campus minister on the West Coast, he knew a young woman who, while she considered herself an agnostic, had always admired her Christian friends because of the disciplines of prayer, Bible study, and fasting they practiced during the season of Lent. Each year during Lent, they prayed regularly, studied Scripture, fasted, and gave up something they enjoyed so that throughout the course of each day, they were reminded of God's claim on their lives as disciples of Jesus Christ. As it so happened, it was Lent when this young woman visited with my friend. "I'm not a Christian," the young woman told him, "but I want to give something up, even though I don't believe in God." My friend thought for a few moments, then came up with a novel idea.

"Why don't you give up your unbelief for Lent? Just for a few weeks, give up agnosticism, and just for these weeks believe and practice the Christian faith. Practice the kind of Christian faith you think Christians ought to practice all the time. Pray just as though you really believe. Read the Bible listening for God to speak to you. And when Lent is over, you can go back to your agnosticism."

So the young woman began practicing the habits of Christian faith. She worshiped. She prayed. She bought a Bible and starting reading it regularly. You can probably predict what happened to her. The young woman "habit-ed" herself right into Christian faith. She started something that she didn't want to stop at the end of Lent. She became a *practicing* Christian.

Often our use of the Psalms—taking a passage from this psalm as a call to worship, using a verse from that psalm in a prayer, quoting a scrap of another psalm out of context to make a point—undercuts the power of the Psalms to fundamentally reshape and form our lives. Using the Psalms in that way forces them into our already fully developed ways of thinking about life and faith. However, the habit of praying the Psalms straight through—*ad seriatim*, day after day, week in and week out, month by month—has the gradual, cumulative effect of relocating us to the Psalms on their own turf, so to speak.

One benefit of developing a habit of praying the Psalms is becoming acquainted with parts of the Psalter we might ordinarily avoid. The habit intensifies the personal nature of our encounter with God in prayer. The habit requires us to hear the questions the Psalms themselves raise rather than just searching them for answers to questions we have already formulated, or worse, searching the Psalms selectively merely to reinforce our existing prejudices. In other words, the habit of regularly praying the Psalms straight through takes us not only deeper into the Psalms but also deeper into the life of the Spirit. Consequently, as we develop a habit of responding to the Word of God, we develop a habit of being in relationship with God.

# I AND THOU IN THE PSALMS

One of the most striking features of the Psalms is their personal nature. The habit of praying the Psalms intensifies this characteristic. Someone (the psalmist) is praying to someone (God) in these psalms, and we are invited into a profoundly moving and intimate personal interchange, a conversation that actually becomes our own through prayer. The one praying believes that the one to whom he or she prays has the power to speak, to respond, and to act. The one praying believes that the one to whom she or he prays has responded in the past and can—and still does—act in the present. The one praying longs for fellowship with God. That person yearns to live in accordance with the expectations of the one to whom she or he prays. The personal directness, the immediacy, and the intimacy of the Psalms are startling. Listen to these lines:

> As a deer longs for flowing streams,
>    so my soul longs for you, O God.
> My soul thirsts for God,
>    for the living God.
> When shall I come and behold
>    the face of God?    —Psalm 42:1-2

> Even though I walk through the darkest valley,
>    I fear no evil;
> for you are with me;
>    your rod and your staff—
>    they comfort me.    —Psalm 23:4-5

42

> *Against you, you alone, have I sinned,*
> *and done what is evil in your sight,*
> *so that you are justified in your sentence*
> *and blameless when you pass judgment.*
> —Psalm 51:4

> *My God, my God, why have you forsaken me?*
> *Why are you so far from helping me, from*
> *the words of my groaning?*
> —Psalm 22:1

> *Bless the* LORD, *O my soul.*
> *O* LORD *my God, you are very great.*
> *You are clothed with honor and majesty,*
> *wrapped in light as with a garment.*
> —Psalm 104:1

In his respected book *I and Thou*, Jewish scholar Martin Buber describes the mystery and intimacy of the relationship between God and humanity. In so doing, he describes the kind of spirituality we find throughout the Psalms.

God, who meets the psalmist as *Thou*, resists all our attempts at reduction or abstraction. Rather, God invites us to speak directly and to have our ideas about God transformed and enlarged in this personal engagement. The God to whom the psalmist speaks as *Thou* cannot be seen yet will be heard. The *Thou*, Buber says, meets us by grace. The *Thou* finds us in our seeking. But the *Thou* cannot be automatically summoned or magically conjured. God is not a product to be consumed. According to Buber, every attempt to reduce God to the category of *it* (even an *Almighty It*) reduces the person praying to *it* too. But the intensely personal spirituality of the Psalms will not permit this to occur. In these prayers, time and again we meet real persons engaged in relationship with God, *I* and *Thou*.[2]

Moreover, the Psalms express this intimacy without diminishing God's holiness, mystery, and transcendence. Indeed, the closer the psalmist draws to God, the greater God appears. When the psalmist speaks of the thoroughness of God's knowledge of him, the experience of being personally searched out in his inmost parts and understood in his innermost thoughts, and when the psalmist describes the relentless presence of God no matter where he flees, he is compelled to cry out to God, "Such knowledge [i.e., knowledge of me by God!] is too wonderful for me; / it is so high that I cannot attain it" (Psalm 139:6).

Those experienced in praying the Psalms bear witness to the transforming power of the *Thou* (the *You*) we meet in these prayers. The Psalms invite each of us to pray as *I* to *Thou*. And when we do pray *I* to *Thou*, we will be compelled to raise the most fundamental questions about ourselves—questions regarding our character, our purpose, and our destiny.

## PSALMS, THE TORAH, AND THE LIVING WAY

Finally, the practice of praying the Psalms brings us into contact with some that are frequently neglected—for example, those that praise God for the Law. Two of these psalms stand out in particular: Psalm 1, the opening psalm of the Psalter; and Psalm 119, the longest psalm in the book (176 verses in all). When we engage in the habit of praying the Psalms, we unavoidably find ourselves immersed in those that extol the Law, or Torah.

In contrast to today's popular religious culture, the Torah psalms reflect the conviction that there are two ways: one leading to life and one leading to death; a way drawing on ageless wisdom handed down for generations in contrast to a way springing up overnight and fading away just as quickly; a way leading to wholeness and a way leading to disintegration; a way building up humanity and a way tearing down humanity. These psalms call forth communities in which persons know and are known, in which life is engendered and meaning is discovered. These psalms remind us that while not everything we learn from tradition may be good, only a fool ignores the collective wisdom of previous generations. While there may be times to stand alone against the community, most of the time it is the voice of the community that should guide and

### Augustine's Confession

"O my God, how I did cry to thee when I read the psalms of David, those hymns of faith, those paeans of devotion which leave no room for swelling pride! ... What cries I used to send up to thee in those songs, and how I was enkindled toward thee by them!"[3]

*(St. Augustine)*

correct. The Torah psalms teach that there is a way to live faithfully and live well together.

I still remember my own lack of appreciation for Psalm 119 when I first began the practice of praying the Psalms. I would dread each month when, from the evening of Day 24 through the evening of Day 26, I would pray Psalm 119. I made my way through what I saw then either as an ode to legalism or as an exercise in clever puzzle-making. (In Hebrew, the entire psalm is arranged as a vast acrostic.) Only as I prayed this psalm for years—and as this habit of prayer led me to inquire *why* the psalmist had devoted so much effort and space to the Law—did I come to a deeper understanding of the significance of the Law and (eventually) of the profound connections between Torah and the way of Jesus Christ. It is often true that the deeper understandings of faith only make themselves available to us gradually over time.

Too often we give up on a practice of faith if it does not instantly yield the desired results; and usually "desired results" means an uptick in our emotional state, a good feeling of some sort, a confirmation of what we already think or believe or want to do. The practice of praying all the Psalms regularly promises no instant spiritual gratification. But it can change our lives—deeply and forever.

So we learn to pray, not all at once but eventually, "You are righteous, O Lord, / and your judgments are right.... Your righteousness is an everlasting righteousness, / and your law is the truth. / Trouble and anguish have come upon me, / but your commandments are my delight. / Your decrees are righteous forever; / give me understanding that I may live" (Psalm 119:137, 142-144).

# INVITATION TO DISCIPLESHIP

Praying the Psalms is a spiritual discipline that, while seldom producing immediate gratification, can be intensely rewarding when practiced over a long period of time. While we may not understand all the themes and sentiments expressed by the psalmists, the questions they evoke can lead us to deeper intimacy with God. At the very least, the Psalms call us to pray. And in a culture that elevates action over reflection, there may be no more counter-cultural Christian practice than to pause and pray.

As Christian disciples, we should be keenly aware that prayer precedes, surrounds, and articulates the goal of all we do; for in prayer we submit our whole lives to God in trust and obedience. The Christian discipline of praying the Psalms daily offers an especially potent practice. But that potency depends on the extent to which we find time to do nothing else but pray; to do nothing else but adore God, praise God, thank God; to do nothing else but express our trust in God, confess our sin to God, and receive forgiveness from God; to do nothing else but place our hope in God and to entrust all our cares to God, interceding with God for the cares of others.

Let us be sure to find time to pray—particularly the Psalms.

# FOR REFLECTION

- Sometimes the Bible teaches us not by answering the questions we have about God or ourselves but by stretching us to ask new questions. Reflect on the psalms you've read so far. Then identify four or five questions you think those psalms pose. How do those questions compare in subject or intent to the questions you ask about God or yourself?

- The Psalms often surprise us with the frankness of their tone. The psalmist expresses grief and anger with as much energy as expressing praise and wonder. How does the frankness of the psalmist challenge and perhaps broaden our conventional understanding of *faith*?

- What does it mean that the open, frank, conversational style of the psalmist is preserved in texts designed primarily for liturgical use?

# The Language of the Heart

*The LORD is your keeper; / the LORD is your shade at your right hand. / The sun shall not strike you by day, / nor the moon by night.*

—*Psalm 121:5-6*

## INTRODUCTION

The Psalms speak through the forms and language of poetry, an evocative language of the human heart. They invite us to participate in them by their very construction, a fact that Claus Westermann observes when he notes that the kind of poetry the Psalms represent is rather different from a purely aesthetic work—in other words, a work of art that exists as an end in itself. Though the Psalms are often stunningly beautiful poetry, beauty is not the target at which they are taking aim. They are not poetry for poetry's sake. Rather, as Westermann explains, the poetry of the Psalms is functional and liturgical. The distinctive rhythms of these poems exist to invite people to worship and pray.[1]

Sadly, with every passing year, it seems more necessary to vindicate the use of poetry as a mode of expression. Such was not always the case. Poetry was once generally accepted as the best way to say something, especially if it was important. If you had an epic story to tell, poetry was your genre. For example, think of Homer's *Iliad* or Milton's *Paradise Lost*. Today the audience for poetry is small and growing ever smaller in comparison to the audiences for novels and popular nonfiction. But there are some things that poetry still does better than any other form of literature.

Poetry stimulates the whole affective realm of human experience better than anything else. Poems speak from and to our feelings; they provoke our emotions. They evoke understandings that lie at an intuitive level of human experience—the inner life or the domain of the heart.

Poetry not only enlivens this level of human understanding, it illuminates this realm of experience, raising it up for reflection, granting us deeper insight into our lives. This week we will read and reflect on the Psalms specifically as *sacred* poetry, as poetry that bears witness to God. In order to do this, we will reverse our usual order of reading first the biblical texts and then reading the commentary. This week, read the commentary first, both to gain a sense of what to look for when reading this specific genre of literature and to gain encouragement and confidence about exploring the Psalms as poetry.

## The Reader as Psalmist

"Word and image coalesce in Psalms. Sound and sight are set on equal footing. Far from dogmatic or abstract, the language of the Psalter is palpably incarnational.... By generating novel associations that open up new vistas of interpretation and application, the metaphor makes the Psalter eminently appropriable for readers in various settings and circumstances. Through the performance of metaphors, the reader becomes the psalmist."[2]

*(William P. Brown)*

# DAILY ASSIGNMENTS

After reading the commentary on Day 1, the instructions for each of the other five days' readings are the same: Read each psalm first in the New Revised Standard Version silently. Then read each Psalm aloud. Poems—and this is especially true of the Psalms—often do not come to life until we read them aloud. Then read each psalm in two other translations, one of which should be the King James Version simply because of its unmatched beauty of verse. The other translation is your choice. Some good options include the New International Version, the New American Standard Bible, the New English Bible, or the TANAKH translation (of the Hebrew Bible). With each translation, read the psalm silently, then aloud.

Since there are two psalms assigned for each day, you may want to read one in the morning and the other in the evening. As appropriate, ask yourself these questions:

- What rhythms of life and language do you discern in the psalm?

- Who is speaking in the psalm? To whom is the psalm addressed?

- How does the familiar become unfamiliar in this psalm? How does the ordinary become sacred?

- What uncomfortable or painful truths are spoken in this psalm?

- What images do you visualize? What beauty of language is expressed in this psalm, and for what purposes?

- What one phrase or word in the psalm do you find most memorable or meaningful?

**DAY ONE:** Read the commentary in the participant book.

**DAY TWO: Psalms 29; 76**

**DAY THREE: Psalms 90; 44**

**DAY FOUR: Psalms 38; 116**

**DAY FIVE: Psalms 37; 103**

**DAY SIX: Psalms 27; 121**

# THE PSALMS AS POETRY

The Psalms are poetry. But approaching the Psalms as poetry does not mean reducing them to nothing *but* poetry. The Psalms are both the words of human writers and the Word of God. Because the Psalms are the Word of God, we listen to them in reverence and trust what God says. Because the Psalms are human words, we listen to them to understand the significance of what the psalmists have to say. And if in our listening we want to understand fully the distinctive message of the Psalms, we should consider how to approach the reading of poetry. A place to start is to realize that while understanding poetry can be hard work, it should never stop being a labor of love.

Poetry can concentrate meaning so intensely that it takes hours, sometimes years, to tease out the insights of a good poem. Poetry can also refract meaning like a verbal prism, making it possible to see a spectrum of insights previously hidden in a single ray of light.

What is crucial to remember is that poems express realities resistant to prose. Like the painter who cannot put it into words what she creates with a brush, the poet expresses thoughts in a poem that she cannot say in prose.

# THE HARD WORK OF LOVE

A good poem invites us into its way of seeing the world. It invites us to see the world through its lenses, to play inside its rhythms and labyrinths, to skip over its surfaces, to let its syllables wash over us, to live with its phrases awhile. A poem is best known from inside the poem's own skin. A poem asks us to engage, enjoy, even struggle to deal with it on its own terms. This is the labor of love, the hard work of understanding poetry.

We have probably all experienced a class in English literature that felt more like a place where autopsies are performed (or where interrogations are conducted) than where life is celebrated. But to understand poetry, we must first appreciate the multiple possibilities of meanings in the stanzas of verse, the occasional slipperiness of words playing with one another, the mazelike quality of the lines, and the ambiguities of texts at play that reflect the even deeper ambiguities of life.

Poems concentrate meanings. Poems layer meanings in a variety of voices. Sometimes a poem deliberately knocks our feet out from under us so we are forced either to see something previously unimagined or to go away without seeing anything at all. Voices may change in the same poem, leaving the reader to wonder, *Who is talking now?* Poems, like Scripture, may change meanings as we change over time, revealing new insights into the world and ourselves. Poetry may not offer us the clarity of a repair manual for the washing machine, but the human heart is far more complex than any kitchen appliance, and what we need requires far more thought.

The shortest distance between two points in the human soul may not be a straight line; it may be a labyrinth. Life is lived in rhythms, like the beat of a heart or the beat of a drum, as least as much as in equations. If we want to hear the Psalms in all their depth and subtleties, we must understand this.

We must also understand more than the meter, rhythm, and rhyme of poetry. Knowing the mechanics of written poetry is not the same as understanding poetry. It is certainly not bad to know about these things. It is just not qualitatively the same thing as getting inside a poem and living it, enjoying it, allowing it to speak to us and (perhaps) speak for us. Even the compulsion to discover "the meaning" of a poem can get in the way of understanding it.

What is my point? Simply this: Poetry often disorients us precisely so that we can be given a new and previously unimagined orientation. Poetry can create dissonance between us and the world around us, and it can make the most ordinary things appear strange and unfamiliar to us. Poetry is especially good at opening our eyes to the holy among the ordinary things of life, so that a common garden or a street or an empty parish church become the stage on which transcendent realities play out. The poets George Herbert and Gerard Manley Hopkins were masters of this. Whether contemplating a piece of church furniture or a shipwreck, they transformed familiar landmarks on the page so that we might with new eyes see eternity among us.

Between the lines of poetry the hidden God is revealed, calling us to trust ourselves to one we cannot conceive. No prose, no matter how good, can quite evoke the human intuition, the creaturely feeling, or the consciousness of our utter reliance on God as well as a good poem can.

Poetry is not hard work for the reader just because it demands attention and imagination. It often makes us face facts about life and ourselves we would like to avoid. It is not easy to be reminded of the daily costs of loss by contemporary poet Wendell Berry. "And yet," he writes, "we all are gathered in this leftover love, / this longing become the measure of a joy all mourners know. / An old man's mind is a graveyard where the dead arise."[3] Easy or not, if we read good poetry, we will confront hard truth.

Finally, poetry can be hard work for the reader because of its density. The way images and ideas are compressed and words are tightly stacked makes it a chore to sort through it all. Poetry revels in language, wonder, beauty, and power of words as much as it revels in wisdom and truth. But the sheer thickness of poetic language can make it hard to digest. For example, listen to Seamus Heaney's "The Rain Stick."

> Up-end the rainstick and what happens next
> Is a music that you never would have known
> To listen for. In a cactus stalk
>
> Downpour, sluice-rush, spillage and backwash
> Come flowing through. You stand there like a pipe
> Being played by water, you shake it again lightly
>
> And diminuendo runs through all its scales
> Like a gutter stopping trickling. And now here comes
> A sprinkle of drops out of the freshened leaves. . . .[4]

The density of the language in a poem like Heaney's is essential to its beauty. The integrity of poetry lies in its language, in its careful structuring of phrases, and in its attentiveness and respect for the word.

# THE PSALMS AS POETRY, THEN AS NOW

So we return to the Psalms. Most of what can be said about good poetry in general can be said of the Psalms as poetry. The Psalms invite us in. In fact, we cannot understand them from the outside. They sometimes make the familiar seem unfamiliar so that they can help us see all things anew. The Psalms certainly can disorient us with no intention of merely restoring us to a former orientation, though when they do, as we shall see, it is our transformation the Psalms have in view.

The Psalms can also be candid to the point of rudeness. They remind us of our sin, accepting no excuses. The Psalms chronicle our suffering and seem to delight in reminding us of our mortality. They come unvarnished and plain-spoken when we would most like them to be diplomatic—if not obscure. The psalmist does not know how to pull any punches when it comes to instructing us in counting our days and taking stock of our frailties. Honesty and directness are chief among the virtues of the Psalms.

The beauty of the language of the Psalms stands in Hebrew and in English translations, and it has survived centuries of good as well as poor scholarship. In Hebrew, the psalmist uses the common poetic devices of parallelism and repetition to stack up images, illuminate ideas, and allow congregations to pray and sing in verses. What may appear at first as mere redundancy is actually the genius of Hebrew poetry. Subtle shades of meaning are disclosed as the psalmist prays, "To you, O LORD, I lift up my soul; / O my God, in you I trust" (Psalm 25:1-2); or, "He alone is my rock and my salvation, / my fortress; I shall never be shaken" (Psalm 62:2). The Psalms demand that we slow down to take them in. Speed reading may help you get through a book on the latest management theory, the psalmist seems to say, but leave your hurries at the door of the Psalter. Here patience is rewarded more than haste.

The spiritual imagination of those of us who grew up on the King James translations of the Psalms is forever enriched by verses from the Psalms like, "Yea, though I walk through the valley of the shadow of death, I will fear no evil: for thou art with me" (Psalm 23:4, KJV); "I will lift up mine eyes unto the hills, from whence cometh my help" (Psalm 121:1, KJV); "I am like a pelican of the wilderness: I am like an owl of the desert. I watch, and am as a sparrow alone upon the house top" (Psalm 102:6-7, KJV). The Psalms invite us to behold the beauty of the Lord, to taste and see that the Lord is good by rel-

## Reading Psalms as Poetry

To grasp fully the message of the psalms of the Bible requires some understanding of their primary poetic features. Two of those features are parallelism and repetition. Parallelism describes the content of one line or verse when it relates to or echoes the content of an adjacent line or verse (for example, Psalm 13:1). Repetition describes the regular recurrence of a word or phrase throughout an entire psalm (for example, Psalm 136).

ishing the flavor of words that convey the Word of God. Though beauty is not the ultimate goal of the Psalms, neither is beauty of language purely incidental to their meaning.

For the next few days, then, we will enter into the Psalms as poetry. As the poet Billy Collins recommends, we will "press an ear against its hive." We will "drop a mouse" into the Psalms "and watch him probe his way out." We will walk inside the Psalms "and feel the walls for a light switch," and maybe just "water-ski across" a few Psalms to feel the waves under our feet.[5]

# INVITATION TO DISCIPLESHIP

"Be still, and know that I am God!" (Psalm 46:10).

Be still so that God's Word can wash over you. Be still so that you can quiet your thrashing, fevered, worried mind, intent on self-justification. Be still so that new understandings can work their way quietly into your heart. Be still so that you can remember you are a creature and God alone is Creator.

Many years ago when I was serving as a hospital chaplaincy intern, our supervisor gave us a wise bit of advice. He said that in a moment of crisis, "Don't just do something; stand there!" The Psalms often advise a similar response. They resist our efforts to rush noisily through their pages. The psalmist loves to slow us down with phrases that turn an idea round and round until every facet catches the light. The psalmist enjoys putting up barriers to quick comprehension, changing voices and tenses and moods to make us stop and change direction and perspective. The psalmist delights in tripping us with unexpected phrases or offensive ideas or previously unimagined images. And when we have picked ourselves up and dusted ourselves off, we are more likely to remember that no disciple can move faster than the master, not if he or she intends to follow.

# FOR REFLECTION

- How has your understanding of the Psalms as poetry affected your understanding of the Psalms you read this week?

- Which specific psalms have held different meanings for you at different times in your life? How do you account for that?

- When or how has your faith been deepened by a psalm that appealed primarily to your affective or emotional sensibilities—in other words, your heart?

- When or how has your faith been deepened by a psalm that appealed primarily to your intellect?

- Which psalms seem most removed from or unrelated to your own life experience? Why do you think that is?

# A Geography of the Imagination

*The heavens are telling the glory of God; / and the firmament proclaims his handiwork. / Day to day pours forth speech, / and night to night declares knowledge. / There is no speech, nor are there words; / their voice is not heard; / yet their voice goes out through all the earth, / and their words to the end of the world.*

*—Psalm 19:1-4*

## INTRODUCTION

Like poetry in general, the Psalms express themselves through powerful images. We began our study with an image *about* the Psalms: We said that when we read, hear, and pray the Psalms, we stand in texts torn asunder by spiritual earthquakes where the promises implicit in God's reign and our experiences of life meet. This image of the Psalms as a center of seismic activity attempts to capture their dynamic character. It reminds us that the Psalms emerged directly from the spiritual struggles of real people. Though in their present form the Psalms have clearly been recrafted into poems and hymns for the use of worshiping communities, we can still sense the personal nature of the struggles represented in them. The Psalms stand in bold relief against the backdrop of creation and history.

There are also many images *in* the Psalms themselves, just as vivid as our earthquake image. These images speak of a world alive with the creative and redemptive presence of God. In fact, the images in the Psalms help us understand what the Psalms are most concerned about and what they are trying to say about who God is and who we are as a people of God. The images provide a window into the theological themes and concerns of the Psalms.

# DAILY ASSIGNMENTS

Pay attention this week in the readings to the images from the created world and from the history of Israel. Mountains spring to their feet to shout praises, and forests give God a standing ovation. History ebbs and flows. Human powers come and go. Kings, armies, chariots, and horses march out to battle, but the results of these battles are not in their power.

Read each psalm silently and then aloud. Listen for the cadences and rhythms of the psalm. Close your eyes to visualize the scenes. In addition to reading the psalms for the day, each day we will read other biblical texts as conversation partners. After reading these other passages, reread the psalms for the day, listening for new insights.

## DAY ONE: Psalms 19; 29

After reading and reflecting on the psalms for the day, read Genesis 1 and 2. Then read the two psalms again.

## DAY TWO: Psalms 46; 107

After reading and reflecting on the psalms for the day, read Revelation 14:1-7 and 22:1-21. Then read the two psalms again.

## DAY THREE: Psalms 74; 77

After reading and reflecting on the psalms for the day, read Job 40 and 41, in which the Lord speaks to Job, and 42:1-6, in which Job answers. Then read the two psalms again.

## DAY FOUR: Psalms 105; 106

After reading and reflecting on the psalms for the day, read Deuteronomy 5 and 6. Then read the two psalms again.

## DAY FIVE: Psalms 74 (again!); 137

After reading and reflecting on the psalms for the day, read 2 Kings 24 and 25 (which chronicles the decline and fall of Judah to Babylon) and Jeremiah 25 (which provides a prophetic reflection on these events). Then read the two psalms again, the first of which reflects the terror of the destruction of Jerusalem, and the second the desolation of exile.

## DAY SIX:

Read the commentary in the participant book.

# IMAGES FROM NATURE

Heaven and earth are on full display in the Psalms. All creation floats like down on the breath of God. All nature responds trembling to God's touch. The fiercest beasts recoil at God's wrath and lie down in obedience to God's command. "When the waters saw you, O God, / when the waters saw you, they were afraid; / the very deep trembled. / The clouds poured out water; / the skies thundered; / your arrows flashed on every side. / The crash of your thunder was in the whirlwind; / your lightnings lit up the world; / the earth trembled and shook" (Psalm 77:16-18).

As powerful as creation is and as vast as the heavens are, according to the Psalms, God is greater still because God is Creator of all that is. But the Psalms are not content to praise merely the almightiness of God, as though power is itself worthy of glorification. The Psalms usher us into the presence of the one whom the Apostles' Creed affirms as "God the Father Almighty." According to the psalmist, the Lord leads the people to "lie down in green pastures," "beside still waters," "through the darkest valley" (Psalm 23). For the psalmist, the human soul becomes "a deer" longing "for flowing streams," thirsting to drink directly from the God who is the source of all life (Psalm 42). Nowhere in all the Bible is the beauty, the power, the glory, and the fundamental wonder of nature so fully on display as in the Psalms. But creation—marvel that it is—*always* points beyond itself to its Creator, demanding a response of reverence and humility from humanity. "When I look at your heavens, the work of your fingers / … what are human beings that you are mindful of them?" (Psalm 8:3-4).

The psalmist seems to live with the insulation stripped from the wires of his soul, exposed to realities many of us take for granted. The psalmist discerns the movement of God's fingers in the ripples on every stream. He evokes, provokes, and compels us to see and listen anew for God in the world around us, this world that God loved into existence and loves still with a divine passion. The images of nature in the Psalms are intended to serve as a portal to a deeper understanding of God, reminding us that nature is good because it was created by God.

# IMAGES FROM
# THE HISTORY OF ISRAEL

The Old Testament turns on two definitive events in the history of Israel: *Exodus* and *Exile*. In the Psalms, these events sometimes fold over one another, one historical moment speaking to another, imbuing present crises faced by the psalmist with as yet unkept promises from the past. As we have already noted, psalms of various historical eras were brought together into a single "book" to be used in the worship of the Jewish people. In fact, as a collection, the Book of Psalms became the hymnbook of the Jewish people after their return from Babylonian exile. As such, the Psalms provided a kind of mountain peak from which to look back over the whole history of Israel from the historical and theological vantage point of the return from exile. From this perspective, the Psalms see the history of Israel as the history of God's faithfulness. They remember the wonders of God's works of creation and redemption, the establishment of an everlasting covenant with Abraham and his descendants, and the deliverance of the children of Israel from slavery in Egypt. The survey of God's history of faithfulness climaxes in the glory of King David's reign and leads us into those dismal and fearful ages that culminate in conquest and exile.

Like all great poetry, the Psalms are concerned with the concrete, the particular. Places and activities become images through which spiritual realities are communicated. Thus, for example, when the Psalms remember the Exodus, it is as though the past event has the power to liberate people from slaveries that threaten them now. Jerusalem—a real city teeming with human population, subject to political and historical shifts and the usual urban problems of bumpy roads and waste disposal— becomes an image of eternal significance: Zion. The Lord's anointed, the Davidic King, takes on significance well beyond the political dimensions of the historical King David himself, symbolizing hope for justice and peace under the reign of God.

## King David

No historical figure of the Bible is more central to the Psalms than King David. With Abraham the patriarch and Moses the deliverer, David the king holds a position of extraordinary symbolic importance in the history of Israel. Warrior, musician, poet, and ruler, David came to the throne after the demise of Saul (c. 1000 BC). The often tragic stories of Saul and David are told in such books of the Bible as First and Second Samuel, First Chronicles, and First Kings.

History and liturgy are brought together repeatedly in the Psalms, allowing the people to articulate their identity in terms of a specific set of events. For example, Psalm 105 recounts the story of the Exodus. Immediately thereafter, Psalm 106 transforms this same story into a kind of litany so that worshipers can participate by remembering. Psalm 106 takes up the story and places it between bookends of praise, providing a historical and theological interpretation to these events, as though to say, "Now, here is the meaning for you of all that happened to your ancestors."

Psalm 106 puts into liturgical practice a principle at stake in the Book of Deuteronomy. For the Jewish people, the event of the Exodus *will not* be relegated to ancient history. The Exodus is a living reality. It exerts God's claim of redemption on every succeeding generation. Indeed, the Exodus becomes the defining reality for the people of Israel. It tells them who they are and to whom they belong. Therefore, according to Deuteronomy, "When your children ask you in time to come, 'What is the meaning of the decrees and the statutes and the ordinances that the LORD our God has commanded you?' then you shall say to your children, 'We were Pharaoh's slaves in Egypt, but the LORD brought us out of Egypt with a mighty hand. The LORD displayed before our eyes great and awesome signs and wonders against Egypt, against Pharaoh and all his household. He brought *us* out from there in order to bring *us* in, to give *us* the land that he promised on oath to *our* ancestors'" (Deuteronomy 6:20-23, italics added for emphasis).

> ## A Psalm Defined
>
> "A psalm is the blessing of the people, the praise of God, the commendation of the multitude, the applause of all…. It softens anger, it gives release from anxiety, it alleviates sorrow; it is protection at night, instruction by day, a shield in time of fear, a feast of holiness, the image of tranquility, a pledge of peace and harmony."[1]
>
> *(St. Ambrose)*

Psalm 106 uses the historical images of the Exodus to make a past event a contemporary one, a living event among the people in their worship. The people praise God for what God has done for their ancestors—and for what God is still now doing for them. The past is not only remembered; it is practiced and enacted in worship. Their history continues to claim the people for God, because the same God who acted long ago acts still.

Psalms 105 and 106 are not alone in using historical images to speak of present spiritual realities. For example, Psalm 95 reflects on a specific incident that occurred after the Hebrew people left Egypt. "O come, let us worship and bow down, / let us kneel before the LORD, our Maker! / For he is our God, / and we are the people of his pasture, / and the sheep of his hand. / O that today you would listen to his voice! / Do not harden your hearts, as at Meribah, / as on the day at Massah in the wilderness, / when your ancestors tested me, / and put me to the proof, though they had seen my work" (Psalm 95:6-9). We are invited here deep into the geography of the imagination in this psalm as historical and theological events merge into a single imaginative reality, a reality that reaches across untold ages to claim the lives of those who pray the psalm. "O come, let us worship and bow down...." In other words, let us not stiffen our necks. We belong to the God who is faithful. According to the psalmist, this is what history teaches us.

It is against the backdrop of God's past faithfulness that the glory of King David's reign stands out so boldly. David is more closely identified with the Psalms than any other person. They are often described simply as the Psalms of David, reflecting his traditional role as author of many of them. Events from David's life often provide the context for particular psalms; whether the events actually gave rise to the particular psalm or whether it was later read back into the event is another matter.

For example, according to the superscription of Psalm 54, this psalm is a prayer for deliverance, "a Maskil of David, when the Ziphites went and told Saul, 'David is in hiding among us.'" The superscription refers us to 1 Samuel 23:19 (also see 1 Samuel 26:1), though the connection between David's story and a particular psalm may have been made by an editor working on a collection of the Psalms.

Given God's faithfulness to David, the magnitude of the king's sin is all the more tragic as a matter of disgrace, a sin of ingratitude against God's overwhelming goodness and abundant mercy to him. The intimacy of David's own personal history with God is virtually unprecedented in the Old Testament. And the breach in that intimacy—when David's lust for Bathsheba leads him to arrange for the death of Uriah—has profound historical consequences. We see these consequences and witness the prophet Nathan's courageous confrontation of David in 2 Samuel 11–12. Psalm 51 articulates David's repentance and renders a set of images, grounded in David's life, that continue to resonate with anyone who prays the Psalms: "Have mercy on me, O God, / according to your steadfast love; / according to your abundant mercy / blot out my transgressions. / Wash me thoroughly from my iniquity, / and cleanse me from my sin" (Psalm 51:1-2).

It is also against the backdrop of God's past faithfulness and of God's mercy that Israel's lament at its destruction gains such force. In Psalm 74, the psalmist remembers God's past faithfulness, deliverance of ancestors, and God's mercy and forgiveness, and then seeks to remind the Lord of the history that God and the people of God share. These historically grounded images reach across the ages and speak wherever people face ruin. "O God, why do you cast us off forever? / Why does your anger smoke against the sheep of your pasture?" (Psalm 74:1).

The history of God's faithfulness fills the people's complaint with a kind of holy rage, and it gives credence to their hope. The psalmist says God has a history of faithfulness with us, so we pray for God to act again on our behalf.

Even when the people are exiled far from home, and even when they are taunted by those who have reduced their cities to ashes, *even then* they will remember their history with God, and their longing for return to Jerusalem becomes a kind of dark hope for God's future. "By the rivers of Babylon— / there we sat down and there we wept / when we remembered Zion.... How could we sing the LORD's song / in a foreign land?" (Psalm 137:1, 4).

The Psalms distill history into poetic images that have the power to transform the present, representing God's past faithfulness as God's claim on our present and future. The energy and the force of the peoples' complaints are grounded in a remembrance of what God has done and of the promises God made for all time to Abraham and his descendants. History appears at many points to be the curse of the Psalms, a bitter reminder and a cruel joke. But history is also the blessing of the Psalter, reminding the people that God reigns. The Psalms refuse to resolve the awful mystery that hangs between the apparent curse and the promised blessing of Israel's history.

# INVITATION TO DISCIPLESHIP

By their very nature, the Psalms reject our attempts at pretense and demand for us to be honest about who we are. They remind us that our identity is grounded in a particular place, in particular relationships, and in a particular time. And they remind us of this by helping us connect our own identity with that of the people of Israel.

"Who are we?" ask the psalmists, again and again. Then they answer, "We are the people who were delivered from slavery. We are the people who wandered in the wilderness. We are the people who were brought into a promised land. We are the people who trusted our own power rather than the Word of God. We are the people who lost their homes and were exiled in a foreign land. We are the people who were restored again to their land by God's gracious hand."

The Psalms will not let our notions of spirituality float off into space. Our life with God is a life with both feet planted on a certain patch of ground, among a very specific community of people, and at a precise moment in history. Understanding this is vitally important for Christians. We are made members of a family of faith through baptism; we are nourished at a common table; we are sustained by sharing the good news of lives touched and changed by God's grace. The Psalms remind us that God is at work through all this human activity in order to keep us from crafting our own likeness into an object of worship.

# FOR REFLECTION

- Those who put together the Psalms intentionally connected the themes of praise, lament, and repentance to situations that occurred in history. Why is it significant that the Bible connects the worship of God with the history of God's people? What implications might there be for your own experience of worship?

- The psalmist pays attention to the smallest details of nature and human experience. What images of nature in the Psalms speak most deeply to you? How might the Psalms correct a Christian spirituality that is disconnected from engagement with the world around us, from ethical obligations, and from our commitments to society?

- To what extent do you think our worship is (or should be) shaped by the concerns for nature, society, and the world at large? What are the dangers of allowing the world to intrude into Christian worship? What are the perils of not allowing it to do so?

- The images of the Exodus and Exile were monumental for the people of Israel. Where have you seen God active in the "exodus and exile" experiences of your own life?

# A Theology of the Imagination

*Ascribe to the LORD, O heavenly beings, / ascribe to the LORD glory and strength. / Ascribe to the LORD the glory of his name; / worship the LORD in holy splendor.... The LORD sits enthroned over the flood; / the LORD sits enthroned as king forever. / May the LORD give strength to his people! / May the LORD bless his people with peace!*

—*Psalm 29:1-2, 10-11*

## INTRODUCTION

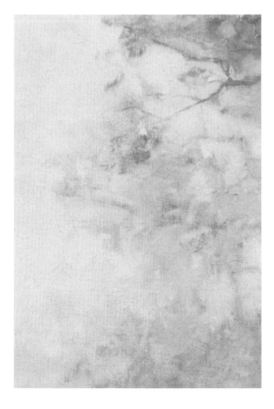

While a royal court is rather foreign territory to most of us reared in an age characterized by nation-states and democracies, it is familiar ground to the biblical text. Unknown to the psalmists is the imaginative furniture of a republic—ballot boxes, constitutions, and branches of government. However, language from the world of kings and subjects runs throughout the Psalms. Yet the language of the royal court is given a theological twist in the Psalms intended to remind us that every human allegiance makes a relative rather than an absolute claim on our loyalties. Only allegiance to God is absolute.

At first glance, we might seem to be on a firmer footing when considering the worship life of the ancient people of Israel, from which so many of the images of the Psalms are drawn. But as we shall see, the Temple of Israel remains remote for most of us. Strange and unfamiliar, images from the Temple are shot through with a wholly and holy otherness that cannot be easily comprehended today. The Psalms we read this week remind us that faith is grounded in profound and impenetrable sanctity and mystery.

With these images from court and temple, we enter into the Holy of Holies of Israel's theological imagination. We sense in the Psalms a struggle taking place for the soul of the people as they wrestle under the rule of kings with the message of the prophets: Worship is reserved for the Lord alone, and worship of God without justice toward humanity is a sacrilege.

# DAILY ASSIGNMENTS

### DAY ONE: Psalms 93; 96; 97; 99

In each of these psalms, the statement "the LORD is king" explicitly occurs. These psalms tell us a great deal about the character of God and the calling of God's people. What do you learn from these psalms about the character of the Lord who reigns? What does it mean to be the subjects of such a king? What does the Lord expect of the people over whom the Lord reigns?

### DAY TWO: Psalms 94; 95; 98

Consider the context of these Scriptures. Why do you think it might be significant that these three psalms are placed among psalms that explicitly speak of the reign of the Lord? To explore this question, first read the three psalms assigned for today. Then go back and read Psalms 93–99, *including* these three psalms. What new ideas and themes are introduced in these three psalms that help us understand the reign of the Lord?

Now read Philippians 2:5-11, an early hymn or psalm to Christ. This hymn describes Christ's self-giving love in humbling himself to become a human being. What parallels and what points of tension do you sense between the understanding of the Lord's power in Psalms 93; 96; 97; and 99 (these were read on Day 1) and in the hymn of the early church recorded in Philippians 2?

## DAY THREE: Psalms 47; 29; 114

Often when we read the New Testament, we hear about "the kingdom of God" and "the kingdom of heaven," phrases that are used interchangeably to speak of God's reign. Read the assigned psalms, and then read Matthew 3:2; 6:33; 18:1-4; and 19:23-26. In what ways do the concepts *kingdom of God* and *God's reign* compare? In what ways do they suggest different understandings or aspects of God's sovereignty?

Kingdoms are not inhabited by citizens but by subjects. What implications might there be in thinking about ourselves as subjects of the Lord who reigns? What are the tensions in the Bible between serving God as a subject and being called children of God? Read Romans 8:14-39, then return to Psalms 47; 29; and 114. What does it mean to be both a subject and an adopted child of the Lord?

## DAY FOUR: Psalms 4; 18; 122

The Temple is portrayed at the heart of the worship of the God of Israel. Read these psalms reflectively, then explore the trajectory of the history that culminated in the Temple by reading Exodus 35–40. Recall that the predecessor to the Temple was the Tabernacle, in which offerings were made to God as the children of Israel wandered in the wilderness.

## DAY FIVE: Psalms 20; 101

While the faith of Israel was indelibly linked to the formal liturgical activities of the Temple, priests and prophets were also teaching that the ethical responsibility of the people was indispensable. Four prophets who brought these ideas powerfully together were Isaiah, Micah, Amos, and Jeremiah. After you have read the psalms for the day, read each of the following texts: Isaiah 6; Micah 6:6-8; Amos 5:18-24; and Jeremiah 31:31-34; 33:1-26. What tensions do the prophets see between worship and ethical responsibility? How might acts of justice and mercy challenge or underscore the worship of God? What difference does it make that those who do justice and love mercy (act ethically) also walk humbly with their God (worship)?

## DAY SIX:

Read the commentary in the participant book.

# IMAGES FROM THE ROYAL COURT

At first glance, it may seem odd to include "Images From the Royal Court" under the heading "A Theology of the Imagination." In fact, however, many of the psalms are theologically unimaginable without the "language world" of the courtly realm.[1] The Psalms portray the Lord as the ultimate king, the "king forever and ever" (Psalms 10:16; see also 29:10), "the LORD of hosts, ... the King of glory" (Psalm 24:10), "the Holy One of Israel" (Psalm 89:18) who reigns over all heaven and earth.

Psalm 2 has "the kings of the earth" (2:2) conspiring against God while the Lord sits on his heavenly throne laughing at them. The psalm culminates with a warning to the earthly kings to "serve the LORD with fear" (2:11), illuminating the meaning of this phrase with the parallel passage telling them they should "with trembling kiss his feet." The picture is of the proud kings of the earth bowing before the heavenly King, lying prostrate in fear and trembling before God's throne. "Why do the nations conspire, / and the peoples

## Psalm Types

Around the turn of the twentieth century, biblical scholar Hermann Gunkel (1862–1932) pioneered an approach to the study of the Book of Psalms that classified each psalm by type, based on common features such as wording, structure, and social or religious life setting. Other scholars added more type categories and subcategories to his initial list. For example:

Hymn, or Song of Praise (Psalm 8); Community Lament (Psalm 44); Individual Lament (Psalm 22); Individual Psalm of Thanksgiving (Psalm 116); Royal Psalm (Psalm 72); Pilgrimage Psalm (Psalm 122); Penitential Psalm (Psalm 51); Song of Trust (Psalm 23)[2]

plot in vain? / The kings of the earth set themselves, / and the rulers take counsel together, / against the LORD and his anointed" (2:1-2). The psalmist responds by basically saying, "What foolishness is this? What vanity? The Lord is king over all kings, ruler over all nations." The Psalms return to this theme repeatedly. It is folly to trust our fate to the princes of the earth, to their armies, to their chariots. The closing of Psalm 2 warns earthly kings to "be wise; / be warned"—in other words, to know the limits of their powers. When the princes of the earth step into the court of the King of heaven, all their earthly power is seen for what it ultimately is: vanity, emptiness.

The Lord reigns not only over the powers of the earth but also over all heavenly powers. The kings of the earth (the highest imaginable and most powerful of mortals) and the heavenly beings themselves bow in the throne room of the Lord. Psalm 29 is what scholars call an "enthronement psalm." In it, the Lord is enthroned above all the chaotic forces he has defeated for the sake of his people. Thus, while Psalm 2 reminds us that God claims our ultimate loyalty and forbids us to give that ultimate allegiance to any earthly powers, Psalm 29 reminds us that the Lord's claim upon our loyalty is comprehensive.

> ## The Lord Reigns
>
> "The psalms are, then, the liturgy of the kingdom of God. The integrity of psalmic speech in all its forms, praise, prayer, and instruction *depends* on the proclamation 'The LORD reigns.'"[3]
>
> *(James L. Mays)*

The Psalms likewise claim that all of life belongs to the Lord and that God's reign extends over all creation. Thus, every human realm and every human power owe allegiance to the Lord, the King of heaven, an idea that remains as resonant today when we sing the hymn "Be Thou My Vision" as it was for ancient Israel. Psalms 93, 96, 97, and 99 explicitly say, "The LORD is king," literally in Hebrew *YHWH malak*, to communicate this core affirmation. The images derive directly from the royal court of kings like David and Solomon: "The LORD is king, he is robed in majesty; / the LORD is robed, he is girded with strength. / He has established the world; it shall never be moved; / your throne is established from of old; / you are from everlasting" (93:1-2). "Say among the nations, 'The LORD is king! / The world is firmly established; it shall never be moved. / He will judge the peoples with equity'" (96:10). "The LORD is king; let the peoples tremble! / He sits enthroned upon the cherubim; let the earth quake!" (99:1). These psalms remind us that everything we are compelled to say in the psalms—whether praise, thanksgiving, or lament—is predicated on this fundamental statement of faith: "The LORD is king."

# IMAGES FROM THE WORSHIP OF THE PEOPLE

As we have already learned, the Psalms are a collection of prayers and hymns and even orders of worship, designed for use by a worshiping community. It should come as no surprise, then, that many of the most powerful images in the Psalms originated in the people's worship of God in the Temple.

For example, Psalm 122 is framed by the image of the Temple standing high in the city of Jerusalem, of worshipers processing toward it. The image is so familiar to Christians as a "call to worship" in our own worship services that we may fail to sense the setting that lies behind these words. The psalm invites us into an ancient rite of pilgrimage, people rejoicing literally in their physical approach to the Temple that crowned the ancient city. Other psalms articulate in various ways the significance of the Temple of Jerusalem, the house of God, wherein dwelled the ark of the covenant (Psalms 80; 99; 102; 135; 138).

Psalm 18 conveys the idea that it is from the Temple itself—the place where sacrifices are offered to God—that God hears the faithful when they pray. "In my distress I called upon the LORD; / to my God I cried for help. / From his temple he heard my voice, / and my cry to him reached his ears" (18:6). The psalm goes on to evoke an image of the presence of God familiar to anyone who has read the first few verses of Isaiah 6. But whereas the canvas on which Isaiah paints is the Temple in Jerusalem, the psalmist paints on a canvas that entails all creation: "Then the earth reeled and rocked; / the foundations also of the mountains trembled / and quaked" (18:7). This psalm mingles images from nature and images from the Temple, utterly transforming both our understanding of what occurs in the Temple and the character of the Lord's actions in the world. Smoke and fire and glowing coals, yes! But now the altar is the earth. Thick darkness stretches beneath God's feet, the heavens, the trembling mountains and quaking earth, drawn together into a liturgy encompassing all creation. Perhaps nowhere more than in Psalm 18 is it so apparent why the Temple is at the heart of the spiritual consciousness of the people of Israel. What occurs at the altar of the Temple is a ritual enactment of a cosmic drama.

It is impossible for us to fully appreciate the sense of holiness the psalmist has when he speaks of the Temple in Jerusalem. What happens in the Temple *really happens*. It is not merely the place where God is thought about, where earnest people express their generalized aspirations or their religious opinions. According to the psalmist, in the Temple, God is "enthroned on the praises of Israel" (Psalm 22:3). God calls forth and receives the sacrifices of the people in the Temple. And it is on the basis of God's remembrance of these sacrifices that God acts on behalf of the people (Psalm 20:2-3). The reverence the psalmist expresses for God is inseparable from the worship offered in the Temple.

The Psalms usher us into this quality of reverence, and they do so precisely by using images from that most holy of all places in the world of ancient Israel, the Temple, where in darkness and fire, in smoke amid the chants of sacred rites, God's priests make sacrifices and offer praise on behalf of all God's people. So when the psalmist speaks of his longing and thirsting for God and asks, "When shall I come and behold / the face of God?" (Psalm 42:2), in the midst of people who scoff at him and ask him, "Where is your God?" (42:3), he responds by saying, "These things I remember, / as I pour out my soul: / how I went with the throng, / and led them in procession to the house of God" (Psalm 42:4).

When the psalmist surveys with wonder the created world—"The earth is the LORD's and all that is in it, / the world, and those who live in it" (Psalm 24:1)—he is compelled not to appeal to the vague pieties of the nature romantic that elevate the creation above the Creator, but to worship a God whose creativity demands reverence and obedience. Thus Psalm 24:3-4 continues: "Who shall ascend the hill of the LORD? / And who shall stand in his holy place? / Those who have clean hands and pure hearts, / who do not lift up their souls to what is false, / and do not swear deceitfully." This psalm moves us from marveling at God's creative handiwork to the doors of the Temple, from a sense of wonder in the presence of the Creator to a realization that the Creator is King over the lives of God's people, and that the King rules all heaven and earth from the Temple.

> ## To Glorify God
>
> "Fully to enjoy is to glorify. In commanding us to glorify Him, God is inviting us to enjoy Him."[4]
>
> (C. S. Lewis)

The Psalms ask, Where does the soul take its struggles? To the worship of God, of course, answer the Psalms, because things really happen there. God really responds. God really acts. Worship really matters, according to the psalmist, because worship is the place where creation's mute cries of praise are gathered up and uttered with a human voice. This is perhaps the most counter-cultural idea to emerge from the Psalms, at least in twenty-first-century North America, where spirituality is often disconnected from the practice of worship in a faith community. When the psalmist's rhetoric soars the highest—"There is a river whose streams make glad the city of God"—the psalmist grounds that soaring vision in the Temple, "the holy habitation of the Most High" (Psalm 46:4). The Temple symbolizes the presence of God; it is a kind of archaeological sacrament reminding the people that "God is in the midst of the city" (Psalm 46:5a).

# INVITATION TO DISCIPLESHIP

Nowhere in the Psalms do the cries of human experience and the claims of divine sovereignty clash more powerfully than around the statement "the LORD is king" (Psalm 93:1). Humanity seems hell-bent on trying to put someone or something other than God in charge of things, that is, on the throne. Indeed, many would prefer to do away with even the language of lordship or kingship when speaking of God. Surely our contemporary bias toward democratic processes (which most of us accept as being a very good thing) should be extended to our doctrine of God, right?

While it is true that there are many wonderful images and metaphors in the Bible describing the character of God—from a just judge to a loving parent to a loyal friend—at our peril we ignore the qualitative difference between God, the Holy One, the Creator, the Preserver, and the Sustainer on the one hand and God's creatures on the other.

But most importantly, this is good news! For in acknowledging that it is the Lord who reigns, we know that we do not. We do not reign over this world. We do not reign over our own lives, and certainly not over the lives of our neighbors. One infinitely and eternally wiser, truer, more compassionate, and more just than we are reigns supreme.

The proclamation from the Psalms is this: "Lift up your hearts" because "the LORD is king." We place our trust in one who is more faithful and trustworthy than any human power. Thanks be to God!

# FOR REFLECTION

- What images and metaphors come to mind when you think about God? Explore the significance of each of these images.

- Although the Psalms provide a variety of ways of thinking about God, drawing on a variety of metaphors, they return repeatedly to the statement "The LORD is king." What seems to be at stake for the psalmist in this phrase? On a personal level, what does it mean for you to say, "The LORD is king"?

- How do you think the psalmist's statement "The LORD is king" relates to the words Jesus gave us to pray, "Our Father which art in heaven, Hallowed be thy name. Thy kingdom come. Thy will be done in earth, as it is in heaven" (Matthew 6:9-10, KJV)?

- Where in your congregation's worship do you see evidence of the lordship of God?

# Lament (and Praise)

*How long, O LORD? Will you forget me forever? / How long will you
hide your face from me? / How long must I bear pain in my soul, /
and have sorrow in my heart all day long? . . . I trusted in your steadfast love; / my heart shall rejoice in your salvation. / I will sing to the
LORD / because he has dealt bountifully with me.*

—Psalm 13:1-2a, 5-6

## INTRODUCTION

We have noted already that there are several types of psalms. In this session, we examine one of the most important of these types: the psalms of lament. Some fifty psalms belong to this type of psalm, in which an individual person cries out to God for help and deliverance. In addition to the individual psalms of lament, there are also communal psalms of lament in which a whole congregation or even the entire people of God cry out.

In this week's readings, we shall encounter those psalms where the enduring promises of God collide with the most troubling aspects of human life, where our remembrance of God's past faithfulness is salt in the open wound of grief and distress. This week we shall pray the psalms that bring comfort to those who feel forsaken by God. And as we pray these psalms of lament, listen: Listen for the word of praise. Listen for changes in voice and inflection as the psalmist moves from complaint and lamentation to thanksgiving and praise. Listen for ways the psalms of lament subvert simplistic or self-serving faith in the name of the Lord, drawing us to know God anew and more deeply. These changes in voice and inflection—from accusation to praise—signal changes in the heart of the psalmist and in the faith of the community.

# DAILY ASSIGNMENTS

The passages for this week are psalms of individual and communal lament from across the Psalter. You have already prayed some of these psalms in other contexts. Now listen to them specifically with reference to the message they convey regarding God's faithfulness in times of trial.

The instructions for daily reading are the same for all five days. First, read each psalm, listening for the changes in the psalmist's voice and inflection and how these changes signal the posture of the psalmist's heart. Then, pray the psalms as your own prayers, allowing them to delve into the hidden heart of lamentation that you may bear, or allowing them to speak on behalf of those around the world who long for deliverance from suffering.

## DAY ONE: Psalms 44; 74; 79

## DAY TWO: Psalms 80; 89

**DAY THREE: Psalms 3; 4; 5; 6; 7; 10; 11; 12**

**DAY FOUR: Psalms 13; 18; 22; 23; 43; 52; 53; 130**

**DAY FIVE: Psalms 40; 41; 42; 55; 56; 71; 102**

**DAY SIX:**

Read the commentary in the participant book.

# ACCEPTING THE PSALMS OF LAMENT

A few years ago, while worshiping in a neighboring congregation, I looked through the condensed selection of biblical texts for worship provided in the back of their hymn book. Among the selections were an abridged Psalter and a variety of Scriptures, mostly from the New Testament, arranged into responsive readings. To my surprise, not only were there no psalms of lament in the Psalter (not even Psalm 22), there were no readings even from the Passion story of Jesus, the heart of the Gospels. The Gospel readings themselves skipped from a few selections from the Sermon on the Mount directly to accounts of Jesus' resurrection. Since that Sunday, I have made it a habit to notice the official and unofficial lectionaries congregations use. Sadly, many churches avoid lamentations and difficult or painful texts of Scripture altogether.

So often we make only the sketchiest use of those parts of the Bible that we find difficult or unpleasant. This is especially true of the psalms of lament. Many Christians are only familiar with psalms like Psalm 133, "How very good and pleasant it is / when kindred live together in unity!" or Psalm 149, "Praise

## Psalms and the Lectionary

Christian congregations that follow a lectionary schedule, such as the Revised Common Lectionary—the calendar of Scripture readings designated for each Sunday of the year—usually include in their order of service a reading from the Old Testament, one from a New Testament epistle, one from a Gospel, and one from the Book of Psalms. The Psalm reading, however, is not simply to be heard alongside the other three, but is intended to be a response to the Old Testament text.

the LORD! / Sing to the LORD a new song, / his praise in the assembly of the faithful." These are great and wonderful psalms, but our faith is impoverished if these are the only psalms with which congregations are familiar. Psalms of lament that call God to account, that point out discrepancies and incongruities in life and faith, and that give voice to the common distresses and pain of human existence are seldom utilized in congregational worship and prayer.

Not only does this approach violate the integrity of the Book of Psalms, but it misunderstands the truth that lies at the heart of the gospel of Jesus Christ, a truth that can be summarized in a single theological observation: The risen and ascended Christ never ceases to bear the scars of crucifixion. We often say there is no Easter Sunday without Good Friday. As true as that statement is, it is also true that Good Friday gives Easter its meaning. Resurrection is not the reversal of a defeat but rather God's stamp of approval on a life lived as God intended.

# WHEN THE BIBLE GETS THE BLUES

You might call the psalms of lament the original blues. We can hear the relentless cadences of the blues emerge in line upon line, while the plaintive voices of psalmists, like singers from the Mississippi Delta, cry out on page after page of these psalms.

The call-and-response pattern of the psalms anticipates the call and response that the blues inherited directly from African American "sorrow songs" of slavery and bond servitude. In his brilliant study *The Souls of Black Folk*, W. E. B. DuBois describes these songs as "the music of . . . the children of disappointment." According to DuBois, sorrow songs such as "Nobody Knows the Trouble I've Seen" and "Roll, Jordan, Roll" represent "the voice of exile." They "tell of death and suffering and unvoiced longing toward a truer world, of misty wanderings and hidden ways."[1] The blues, sung by Muddy Waters, Buddy Guy, and scores of other men and women, is the secular child of these sorrow songs.

In many of the sorrow songs and in so much of the blues, we hear the pain of dislocation, the wail of personal and social anguish, and the longing for deliverance. We hear much the same in the great psalm of exile, Psalm 137, which begins, "By the rivers of Babylon— / there we sat down and there we wept / when we remembered Zion. / On the willows there / we hung up our harps. / For there our captors / asked us for songs, / and our tormentors asked for mirth, saying, / 'Sing us one of the songs of Zion!' / How could we sing the Lord's song / in a foreign land?" The taunting of their oppressors only compounds the dislocation of the people, forcibly removed from their homes to a strange land.

The Psalms are distinctively Hebrew in so many ways, but at some level the psalms of lament reflect something common to all humanity. People everywhere know what it means to long for the safety of those they love, for trustworthiness in their friends, for respect from their neighbors. People everywhere know what it means to yearn for justice and peace in a dangerous world. People everywhere have felt the sting of bigotry, of exclusion, of exile, the sorrow of not belonging, the ache of promises unkept, the yearning for God to remember them. Such yearnings are not restricted to any particular ethnic group, nationality, or religion.

Just being alive is enough to make us long for wholeness in life. Just paying attention to life can evoke lamentations from us. However, the full force of the

## Musical Instruments in the Bible

Musical instruments played a crucial role in the worship life of the people of ancient Israel. Stringed instruments made of wood such as the *kinnor* (translated as "lyre" in the TANAKH or "harp" in the NRSV) were played by King David. According to Psalm 137:2, Jewish exiles hung these instruments on the branches of the trees by the rivers of Babylon when they could not sing the Lord's song in a foreign land.

Similar to the kinnor were the harp (Psalm 33:2) and the lute (Psalm 92:3). Wind instruments included the flute (Psalm 5, superscription) and the trumpet (Psalm 81:3). Percussion instruments included the tambourine (Psalm 68:25) and cymbals (Psalm 150:5).[2]

psalms of lament derives from a specific history of God's dealings with a particular people, Israel. "We have heard with our ears, O God, / our ancestors have told us, / what deeds you performed in their days, / in the days of old" (Psalm 44:1). The people were told the stories of God's past deliverance as their own stories. They handed down the stories from one generation to another. The retelling of this history made the people who they were. It formed them as a people, formed by the Exile and the Exodus, formed to live on the strength of God's promise.

Through ages of suffering and slavery and times of deliverance, rebellion, and redemption, these people chronicled the faithfulness of God. The history of God's faithfulness forms the backdrop for the psalms of lament. This history also provides the grounds for the people's complaint against God and ultimately for their hope for the future. They ask the Lord, "O God, why do you cast us off forever? / Why does your anger smoke against the sheep of your pasture? / Remember your congregation, which you acquired long ago, / which you redeemed to be the tribe of your heritage" (Psalm 74:1-2). They remind God of the covenant as they petition him: "Yet God my King is from of old, / working salvation in the earth.... Have regard for your covenant, / for the dark places of the land are full of the haunts of violence. / Do not let the downtrodden be put to shame; / let the poor and needy praise your name" (Psalm 74:12, 20-21). Without the history of God's faithfulness, the people's laments lack their essential force. Because of this history, their laments become theologically inevitable.

At times, the psalms of lament provide a kind of liturgical response to the message of Israel's prophets, like Hosea, in which a feckless and faithless people pray to the Lord, and the Lord says to these people who had disowned their God, "You are my people," and the people respond, "You are my God" (Hosea 2:23). At other times, the psalms of lament stand as the testimony of those innocent victims of history who suffer violence and exile, and who raise their fist toward heaven demanding God's justice in the face of human cruelty.

# SUBVERSIVE RHYTHMS

Old Testament scholar Walter Brueggemann has observed that the psalms of lament move the worshiper from a *past orientation*—in which life and faith were settled and taken for granted—through a time of profound *disorientation*—when danger and loss overtake the psalmist—and toward a *new orientation*—where faith must expand or be transformed to take account of God's purposes in light of the difficulties we have faced.[3] The movement of the psalms of lament, from a remembered past orientation through an experience of disorientation and toward a new orientation, represents an unsettling, even a subversive rhythm at the heart of the Psalter.

Each psalm of lament reflects some aspects of this rhythm, and a few reflect all aspects. As each psalm of lament opens, it speaks in the wake of some disorienting experience, but it assumes a prior time of orientation. Brueggemann describes this prior condition of orientation as consisting of "being well-settled, knowing that life makes sense and God is well placed in heaven, presiding but not bothering.... In terms of the Bible, this attitude of equilibrium and safe orientation is best reflected in the teaching of the old Proverbs which affirm that life is equitable, symmetrical, and well-proportioned."[4] There are passages in the Psalms that reflect essentially this view of the world. For example, Psalm 37:25: "I have been young, and now am old, / yet I have not seen the righteous forsaken / or their children begging bread."

Most of us enjoy those times when life feels settled and under some semblance of control. But while an experience of orientation or equilibrium can be a real blessing, Brueggemann points out that a people's state of orientation can merely serve to confirm the conventional, the status quo, our preference for coherence, consensus, and order at the expense of the prophetic, the new, and the visionary. The condition of orientation can be a problem at a level of personal spirituality and at the level of an entire society.

Those who are familiar with the psychological dynamics of crisis will recognize the realities described in the psalms of lament. It is frequently true that in the midst of life crises, people confront and reevaluate long-settled questions of ultimate meaning: during an experience of profound grief after the death of a loved one, amid the wreckage of divorce, after the loss of a career that provided significant meaning as well as income, in the dissolution of an old friendship when confidence lies shattered, or in the wake of a major life-threatening illness as basic physical capacities are compromised.

One error we can often make in our interpretation of the psalms of lament is to see in them only a movement from orientation to disorientation and finally to reorientation. In truth, reorientation of perspective or life situation may not be what the psalmist gets. If the psalmist grows through the experience of disorientation, he may discover a *new* orientation, not just a reorientation to his previous condition and his prior understanding of God and the world. The psalmist learns to sing a *new song* unto the Lord.

The psalms of lament—especially individual psalms of lament—often map the course of a life transformed in the crucible of suffering. The change is not only psychological; it is also spiritual, representing fundamental shifts in our way of understanding God's relationship to the world and our relationship to God. Perhaps the person of faith discovers that the king's desires and God's will are not synonymous. Perhaps the person of faith discovers that sometimes the faithful suffer through no fault of their own, that the rain from heaven falls on the just and the unjust. Perhaps the person of faith discovers that God's grace is not restricted to those who share one's views about God and one's moral values. The psalms of lament stand as testimony to the fact that the Lord is a living God, and sometimes following the Lord involves a sprint and not a leisurely stroll, even though the course we are running is long, with lots of twists, turns, ups, and downs.

# QUESTIONS AND ANSWERS?

If the Lord reigns, why do good people suffer? If the Lord reigns, why do injustice and violence continue? The psalms of lament exist because people of faith—people who trust God, people who know the story of God's faithfulness as their own history—refuse to close their eyes to the world around them. They meet life realistically, and they interrogate God. The nation is overrun, the temple lies in ruins, the people are driven into exile, and yet the Lord still reigns? The psalmist holds God ultimately accountable for the world in which we find ourselves, because the psalmist truly believes the Lord reigns.

The psalms of lament grab God by the lapels, eye to eye and face to face, and demand to know, "Where are you, Lord? Have you forsaken me forever?" These psalms are personal prayers, sometimes angry tirades or chronicles of grief. At times overflowing with regret, at times steeped in the psalmist's feelings of having been personally wronged by God, they are nonetheless faithful prayers. The psalms of lament invite us into a faith that, for us as Christians, cannot rest until it embraces the incarnation of God in Jesus Christ. They cling to the trust that refuses to believe that God is too small to be held accountable. These psalms hold to the hope against hope that the seismic stresses caused by our confidence in God's reign and our experience of the terrors and risks of human existence can be held together, *but only by God*. The world God created bears witness that God loves freedom more than safety, and the psalms of lament never cease to hold God responsible for the dangerous world in which we live. They confirm that life's terrors are inseparable from life's wonders, and sorrow is the price tag on everything we love. Lament is woven into the fabric of life by inevitability's loom, but lamentation can never be far from praise.

# INVITATION TO DISCIPLESHIP

Transformation is the child of turbulence. We seldom grow in settled circumstances. Certainly this is one of the enduring lessons of the psalms of lament; and the implications are inescapable for people of faith. In moments of crisis—when the old wine skins we have carried for years burst because of the pressure of new wine—we usually discover that our faith is inadequate, that our God is too small.

The story of the people of Israel unfolds from one crisis to another, as they are challenged to trust an ever-larger God: from their exodus out from Egyptian bondage into the terrible freedom of wandering; from the wilderness experience to a promised land that was given but still had to be won; from the time of the judges to the age of kings; from security to exile and home again. Along the way, the pilgrim people discovered the pilgrim God.

Perhaps it is only human to long for the absence of conflict and crisis. No garden can grow if perpetually harrowed. But it is just as true that no garden will grow in earth unturned by the plow.

The psalms of lament encourage us to keep our faith during times of conflict and crisis precisely by giving us permission to hold God accountable for the terrible and wonderful freedom woven into God's creation. While hard or perhaps even impossible to understand, the trials of life invite us into closer communion with the God who suffers with us and who promises life beyond every death.

# FOR REFLECTION

- It is in the psalms of lament that Scripture often becomes most personal. Most of us have had experiences in which we have prayed for God to deliver us or someone we love from misfortune and pain. Most of us have struggled with the experience of prayers that either have not been answered or have been answered in ways that contradicted our hopes. When have your own experiences of pain and loss driven you to lament to God?

- Congregations too often neglect the psalms of lament in corporate worship, preferring psalms that celebrate the status quo. What is lost in our avoidance of communal lamentation? What might we be afraid of confronting if we were to engage the psalms of lament? What potential depths and riches of faith might open up to us if we did indeed open our hearts to God in lamentation? How might our congregations make better and fuller use of the psalms of lament?

- What does it mean to you personally to know that God is willing and ready to hear from you, even when all you can express is grief, loss, fear, anger, or pain?

- Recall the commentary's description of Walter Brueggemann's categories of *past orientation, disorientation,* and *new orientation* (see pages 85–87). Reflect on an experience you have had of moving from orientation to disorientation and finally to new orientation.

# Grace and Repentance

*Have mercy on me, O God, / according to your steadfast love; /
according to your abundant mercy / blot out my transgressions. /
Wash me thoroughly from my iniquity, / and cleanse me from my sin. /
For I know my transgressions, / and my sin is ever before me.*

—*Psalm 51:1-3*

## INTRODUCTION

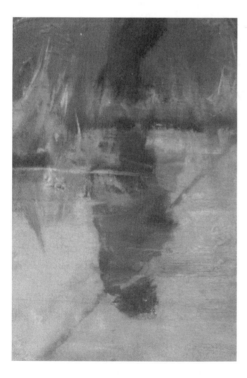

No psalms are more relevant to our needs than the penitential psalms. It is in these psalms that the psalmist cries out for the mercy of God and seeks God's forgiveness. Psalm 51, the most memorable of these, is closely tied to the story of King David. Other penitential psalms (Psalms 6; 32; 38; and 143) are also attributed in their superscriptions to David. One penitential psalm (Psalm 102) is attributed poignantly to "one afflicted, when faint and pleading before the LORD," while another (Psalm 130) is "a Song of Ascent," one of a collection of psalms used in the pilgrimage of the faithful "up" to Jerusalem. Whatever the occasions of authorship or the purposes for which these psalms were originally intended, they remain wonderfully adaptive to the needs of the faithful in every age.

91

It is altogether appropriate, then, that our engagement with these psalms of repentance should take place in the context of our own spiritual self-examination. To that end, the assignments for reading and praying the Psalms this week will be framed within a traditional penitential service. Each day's reading will be contained within this brief service of worship and designed to promote reflection on the meaning of the assigned psalms as well as upon our own relationship to God.

# DAILY ASSIGNMENTS

The prayers for the penitential service of worship printed below are drawn from the Ash Wednesday service in the Book of Common Prayer.[1] The order of worship is an invitation to thoughtful reflection on the mercy of God and the spiritual dimensions of the lives we lead. Be careful not to rush through it. During Days 1–5, your assignment each day will be to read through the penitential service below. Some elements of the service will be the same every time. Other elements—the first hymn, the Psalter reading, the Scripture reading, and the last hymn—will list something different for each of the five days. Consider reading the complete service aloud at least one of the days, and try to sing some of the hymn selections. On Day 6 you will read the commentary in the participant's book.

## PENITENTIAL SERVICE

### Opening Sentences

"All we like sheep have gone astray; / we have all turned to our own way; / and the LORD has laid on him / the iniquity of us all" (Isaiah 53:6).

(Silent reflection)

"I will get up and go to my father, and I will say to him, 'Father, I have sinned against heaven and before you; I am no longer worthy to be called your son'" (Luke 15:18-19).

(Silent reflection)

### Call to Worship

"O Lord, open my lips,
    and my mouth will declare your praise.
For you have no delight in sacrifice;
    if I were to give a burnt offering, you would not be pleased.

The sacrifice acceptable to God is a broken spirit;
a broken and contrite heart, O God, you will not despise" (Psalm 51:15-17).

## Prayer

"Almighty and everlasting God, you hate nothing you have made and forgive the sins of all who are penitent: Create and make in us new and contrite hearts, that we, worthily lamenting our sins and acknowledging our wretchedness, may obtain of you, the God of all mercy, perfect remission and forgiveness; through Jesus Christ our Lord, who lives and reigns with you and the Holy Spirit, one God, for ever and ever. *Amen.*"

## Hymn

Sing or meditate in silence on one of the following texts, as assigned for each day of the week. The hymns may be found in a wide range of denominational hymnals.

**DAY ONE: "Just As I Am, Without One Plea"**

**DAY TWO: "Out of the Depths I Cry to You"**

**DAY THREE: "How Firm a Foundation"**

**DAY FOUR: "Great Is Thy Faithfulness"**

**DAY FIVE: "Pass Me Not, O Gentle Savior"**

## Psalter

Psalm(s) of penitence are assigned for each day in your daily assignment. Pray the assigned psalm(s) as your own prayer of penitence. Then reflect in silence.

**DAY ONE: Psalm 102**

**DAY TWO: Psalms 6; 32**

**DAY THREE: Psalm 38; 143**

**DAY FOUR: Psalms 130**

**DAY FIVE: Psalm 51**

## Scripture

Biblical texts are assigned for this day in your daily assignment. Read the assigned biblical text. Then reflect in silence.

**DAY ONE: Isaiah 58**

**DAY TWO: Luke 15**

**DAY THREE: Luke 18**

**DAY FOUR: Romans 3:9-26**

**DAY FIVE: 2 Samuel 12**

## Call to Confession

"If we say that we have no sin, we deceive ourselves, and the truth is not in us. If we confess our sins, he who is faithful and just will forgive us our sins and cleanse us from all unrighteousness" (1 John 1:8-9).

## Prayer of Confession

"Most holy and merciful Father: We confess to you and to one another, and to the whole communion of saints in heaven and on earth, that we have sinned by our own fault in thought, word, and deed; by what we have done, and by what we have left undone."

*Lord, hear us as we pray.*

"We have not loved you with our whole heart, and mind, and strength. We have not loved our neighbors as ourselves. We have not forgiven others, as we have been forgiven."

*Have mercy on us, Lord.*

"We have been deaf to your call to serve, as Christ served us. We have not been true to the mind of Christ. We have grieved your Holy Spirit."

*Have mercy on us, Lord.*

"We confess to you, Lord, all our past unfaithfulness: the pride, hypocrisy, and impatience of our lives,"

*We confess to you, Lord.*

"Our self-indulgent appetites and ways, and our exploitation of other people,"

*We confess to you, Lord.*

"Our anger at our own frustration, and our envy of those more fortunate than ourselves,"

*We confess to you, Lord.*

"Our intemperate love of worldly goods and comforts, and our dishonesty in daily life and work,"

*We confess to you, Lord.*

"Our negligence in prayer and worship, and our failure to commend the faith that is in us,"

*We confess to you, Lord.*

"Accept our repentance, Lord, for the wrongs we have done: for our blindness to human need and suffering, and our indifference to injustice and cruelty,"

*Accept our repentance, Lord.*

"For all false judgments, for uncharitable thoughts toward our neighbors, and for our prejudice and contempt toward those who differ from us,"

*Accept our repentance, Lord.*

"For our waste and pollution of your creation, and our lack of concern for those who come after us,"

*Accept our repentance, Lord.*

"Restore us, good Lord, and let your anger depart from us;"

*Favorably hear us, for your mercy is great.*

"Accomplish in us the work of your salvation,"

*That we may show forth your glory in the world.*

"By the cross and passion of your Son our Lord,"

*Bring us with all your saints to the joy of his resurrection.*

(Silent reflection)

## Hymn

Sing or meditate each day on one of the following texts, as assigned for each day of the week. The hymns may be found in a wide range of denominational hymnals.

**DAY ONE: "Amazing Grace"**

**DAY TWO: "I Need Thee Every Hour"**

**DAY THREE: "Jesus, the Very Thought of Thee"**

**DAY FOUR: "Come, Thou Fount of Every Blessing"**

**DAY FIVE: "All Hail the Power of Jesus' Name"**

## Closing Prayer

"Almighty God, who hast given us grace at this time with one accord to make our common supplication unto thee, and hast promised through thy well-beloved Son that when two or three are gathered in his Name thou wilt be in the midst of them: Fulfill now, O Lord, the desires and petitions of thy servants as may be best for us; granting us in this world knowledge of thy truth, and in the world to come life everlasting. *Amen.*" (A Prayer of St. Chrysostom)

## NOTES

**DAY ONE:**

**DAY TWO:**

**DAY THREE:**




**DAY FOUR:**




**DAY FIVE:**




**DAY SIX:** Read the commentary in the participant book.

# CALLED TO REPENTANCE

My friend had just dropped me off after we had lunch together. He was serving as the senior pastor of a bustling suburban congregation, and under his leadership the church had turned around after several years of declining membership to become one of the fastest-growing congregations in our region. He was justifiably proud of the work he and his staff had done. Perhaps this is why what he said shocked me so: "I've decided to take the 'corporate confession of sin' out of the Sunday worship service. It's such a downer for the people to do that every Sunday."

## The Book of Common Prayer

The Book of Common Prayer (BCP) was a product of the sixteenth century Protestant Reformation. Its first version, largely the effort of Thomas Cranmer, the Archbishop of Canterbury, appeared in 1549. Over the centuries and through many editions, the services, collects, daily prayers, and the schedule for praying through the Psalms monthly have shaped the lives of countless Christians.

What could be any more a "downer" than for God's people to leave worship every week without having confessed their sin and been assured of God's mercy? Indeed, there are few spiritual needs more profound than the need to confess our sin and to be reminded of (and accept) God's forgiveness. The Book of Psalms reflects this need, providing us not only with a collection of psalms specifically dedicated to repentance, but also with penitential elements woven throughout. Psalm 39:5b-8a reminds us, "Surely everyone stands as a mere breath. / Surely everyone goes about like a shadow.... And now, O Lord, what do I wait for? / My hope is in you. / Deliver me from my transgressions."

The Psalms reflect a spiritual sanity utterly contrary to a spirit of self-righteousness. The penitential psalms remind us that we are not called to judge the shortcomings of others and to congratulate ourselves for our own morality. We are called to bow before God, who alone is holy and righteous, who alone judges rightly, and to confess our sin to God and in the presence of one another. Why was it that throughout his public ministry, Jesus reserved his harshest criticism not for a woman caught in adultery or for tax collectors but for the most spiritually minded members of his own faith? The answer, at least in part, lies in the Psalms, which tell us repeatedly that there is none righteous but God alone. While God is eternal, enduring forever and ever, humanity wears out like a garment, withers like grass, passes away into the dust of history. God's justice is absolute. God's mercy is beyond measure. God's knowledge of us is complete and comprehensive. By contrast, our understanding is fleeting. Our knowledge even of ourselves is flawed, our discernment of the hearts of others is negligible, and our duty lies in reverence toward God and respect of others. In comparison to God, not even the most righteous human being looks very good.

> ## Saying the Psalms Aloud
>
> "To say or sing the psalms aloud within a community is to recover religion as an oral tradition, restoring to our mouths words that have been snatched from our tongues and relegated to the page, words that have been privatized and effectively silenced."[2]
>
> (Kathleen Norris)

## WHATEVER BECAME OF SIN?

In 1973, psychiatrist Karl Menninger asked, "Whatever became of sin?" and the question remains as provocative today as when he originally asked it. In fact, perhaps it is even more provocative today because the word *sin* is used more and more in our time to designate what we do not approve of in others rather than to name our own wrongdoings.

Perhaps there has never been a better time than now to recover the confession of sin that some of us learned as children:

> *Almighty and most merciful Father, we have erred and strayed from thy ways like lost sheep, we have followed too much the devices and desires of our own hearts, we have offended against thy holy laws, we have left undone those things which we ought to have done, and we have done those things which we ought not to have done.*[3]

Certainly, this prayer places the responsibility for sin at our own doorstep rather than at trying to shift the blame to someone else.

The penitential psalms help us understand the personal dimensions of sin by the various shades of meaning they convey, using slightly different words to describe that from which the psalmist repents. For example, as scholar Samuel Terrien observes, Psalm 51 uses three synonyms: transgressions, iniquity, and sin. He explains, "The word 'transgressions' refers to acts of rebellion and of willful revolt committed against the law. 'Iniquity' designates a state of distortion, bending, or twisting, which vitiates the whole outlook and therefore the subsequent behavior of a [person]."[4] Finally, the word "*sin*, in Hebrew as well as in Greek, is the missing of the mark, the falling short of the goal, the incapacity to reach one's end, the failure to fulfill one's destiny. A sinner is merely a [person] who has never learned how to live."[5]

At its heart, sin consists in our refusal to love and to be loved. Sadly, however, even the word *love* has fallen on hard times too. It has come to mean little more than romantic infatuation or some vague generalized good feeling toward others. From the perspective of Christian theology, love is grounded in the character of God, specifically in God's unimaginable power of self-surrender and God's inexhaustible self-giving.

Only by taking seriously the character of a God who is love can we understand what it means to repent. We turn toward God because we have the confidence that God loves us, that God has forgiven us fully and forever. We turn from sin because we know that sin separates us from the fullness of our humanity and from that communion with God and others, which God created us for and without which we shall never be whole.

The penitential psalms understand implicitly that sin disintegrates. Whether in the pride of self-righteousness or the violence of self-centeredness, sin separates and alienates. There is no such thing as faithful humanity in isolation, not if humanity is created in the image of the God who is a Holy Communion of Father, Son, and Holy Spirit. Therefore, when God calls us to repent, God draws us into community. The penitential psalms understand this: "Let this be recorded for a generation to come, / so that a people yet unborn may praise the LORD . . . so that the name of the LORD may be declared in Zion, / and his praise in Jerusalem, / when peoples gather together, / and kingdoms, to worship the LORD" (Psalm 102:18, 21-22). The Pharisee may stand alone to pray; the older brother may refuse to attend the party his father gives in honor of the prodigal's return; the haughty, the arrogant, and the violent may place themselves and their interests above the needs of others; but the way of repentance leads us to bow *together*, to pray *together*, and ultimately to live *together*.

# FORGIVENESS AND REPENTANCE

Repentance includes remorse, our feeling sorry for our sin. But repentance is much more than that. It means to turn around, to turn fully from one direction to another. Repentance requires surrender to God's direction for our lives. It certainly does not mean claiming God's endorsement for our views. Humility is as essential to repentance as silence is to reverence and trust is to faith. The father cried out to Jesus, "[Lord,] I believe; help my unbelief!" (Mark 9:24). The penitent cries out, "Lord, I repent; show me which way to turn."

I suspect it is not fear of our past sins that keeps us from repenting but rather anxiety for the future. We resist turning to God not because we are afraid of what God will think about what we have done. Rather, we resist repentance because we are afraid of where God might lead us or what God might call us to do. This is why the definitive penitential psalm (Psalm 51) includes the psalmist's vowing to teach others and to praise God. The repentant sinner in the psalm does not just turn around and stand still; he turns around and moves into a new future. The repentant sinner does not just want to be delivered from the consequences of his sin; he wants to be delivered from the sin itself into a new life. Repentance is about learning to live well, to become who God created us to be.

On this point, the understanding of sin as reflected in the Psalms and in the prophets of ancient Israel was miles ahead of every pagan religion that surrounded them. For the pagan religions, sin was a religious or cultic matter. But for the psalmist and the prophets, sin was a matter of life and death. In their understanding, sin had ethical and moral dimensions. In other words, the God of the Hebrews did not covenant with his people to make them more religious, but to make them fully human. This is why Psalm 51 contrasts the cultic presentation of burnt offerings with "the sacrifice acceptable to God," which is "a broken spirit; a broken and contrite heart" (51:16-17).

However, in light of the teachings of Jesus, the penitential psalms may take us even farther as Christians. The Psalms have a rich understanding of the moral dimensions of the sin from which we are called to repent. But the model that predominates in the Psalms is what might be called "*legal* repentance." In the penitential psalms, there is a view of repentance that essentially says, "Repent, and *if* you repent, *then* you will be forgiven." God's forgiveness appears to be dependent upon our repenting—and repenting sincerely and adequately. Repentance in the penitential psalms is "legal," in others words, in that it is seen as a work we do in order to earn forgiveness or to make God act graciously toward us.

In contrast to this idea of legal repentance, the New Testament presents what some Protestant Reformers described as *"evangelical* repentance"—that is, the view that God's forgiveness of us is prior to our repentance.[6] The fact that God forgives us, the fact that God is gracious and merciful toward us, makes it possible for us to turn to God in repentance. Specifically the word *evangelical* here refers to Jesus' revolutionary teachings on God's forgiveness.

For us as Christians, we should also hear the penitential psalms through the gospel of Jesus Christ. We are compelled to hear the psalmist's cry, "Have mercy on me, O God, / according to your steadfast love; / according to your abundant mercy / blot out my transgressions. / Wash me thoroughly from my iniquity, / and cleanse me from my sin" (Psalm 51:1-2), as a cry on the lips of the prodigal who "comes to himself" and who says, "I will get up and go to my father, and I will say to him, 'Father, I have sinned against heaven and before you'" (Luke 15:18). It is crucial to understand the movement of grace in these passages, which makes it possible for the psalmist and the prodigal to repent. God's forgiveness was prior to the repentance of the prodigal. In loving kindness, mercy, and grace, God longed and looked for the prodigal's return. When the son was yet far off, the father ran out to meet him. And when the prodigal went into his prepared speech, begging for mercy, the father was already embracing and kissing him. For Jesus, it is clearly not the adequacy of our repentance that makes God gracious; it is the adequacy of God's forgiveness that makes us repent.

So when we read the penitential psalms, let us hear them through Jesus Christ. God is like a shepherd who will not sleep until he recovers the one sheep that has wandered off into the wilderness and is in danger of being eaten by wolves. God is like a woman who will not rest until she finds her lost coin. God is like a father who loves and forgives his children, who waits for the prodigal to return, and who pleads with the older son to rejoice in the restoration of communion with his brother. Let us repent even of our understanding of repentance. Then we may hear with joy, "Happy are those whose transgression is forgiven, / whose sin is covered" (Psalm 32:1). We can repent and live in confidence and joy, because God has forgiven us fully and forever in Jesus Christ.

# INVITATION TO DISCIPLESHIP

If, according to Samuel Terrien, a sinner is "merely a [person] who has never learned how to live,"[7] then there are two sides to a major theme running throughout the penitential psalms, one retrospective and the other prospective. Both relate to what it means to learn "how to live."

On the retrospective side, these psalms call us to recognize ourselves for what we are: sinners. We are called to utter this simple prayer: "God, be merciful to me, a sinner!" (Luke 18:13). The great distinctive of the church consists simply in this stunning awareness, that we are all sinners forgiven by the mercy of God. The great challenge for the church consists in never forgetting the reality of our sinfulness and never presuming our sinfulness to be stronger than God's mercy.

On the prospective side, we are called to live gratefully into the humanity for which God created us and set us free in Christ. It is so easy to forget that God did not go to all the trouble of Creation and Incarnation just to make us more religious but rather to make us more human. This is why it is vital to keep before us the story of God in Israel as well as the story of God in Christ Jesus if we are to understand what it means to repent.

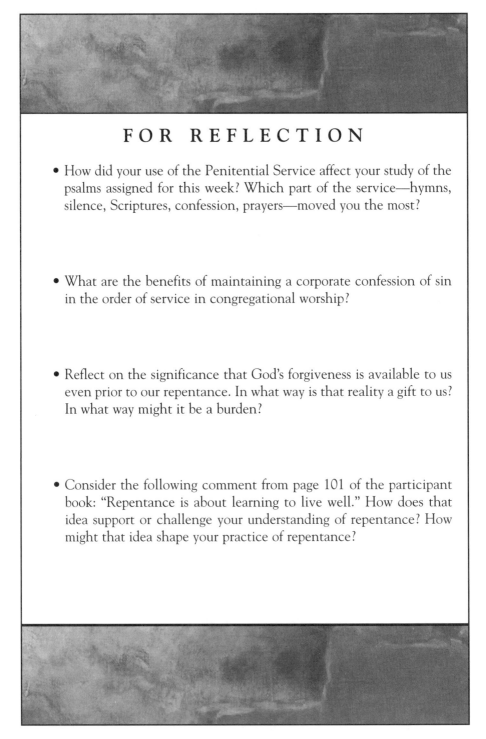

# FOR REFLECTION

- How did your use of the Penitential Service affect your study of the psalms assigned for this week? Which part of the service—hymns, silence, Scriptures, confession, prayers—moved you the most?

- What are the benefits of maintaining a corporate confession of sin in the order of service in congregational worship?

- Reflect on the significance that God's forgiveness is available to us even prior to our repentance. In what way is that reality a gift to us? In what way might it be a burden?

- Consider the following comment from page 101 of the participant book: "Repentance is about learning to live well." How does that idea support or challenge your understanding of repentance? How might that idea shape your practice of repentance?

# Love and Wrath

*O LORD, you God of vengeance, / you God of vengeance, shine forth!*
*/ Rise up, O judge of the earth; / give to the proud what they deserve!*

—Psalm 94:1-2

## INTRODUCTION

The psalms of wrath or vengeance, which scholars refer to as the imprecatory psalms, represent the most difficult ones for Christians to pray. These psalms express the sheer power of moral outrage, both a visceral reaction against perceived wrongs and an urgent desire for divine intervention. They also remind us of the danger to our own souls and the peril to the lives of others when we possess moral indignation without the accompanying virtues of humility and mercy.

The categorical certainty with which these psalms distinguish between good and bad people, between the "righteous" and "evildoers," articulates a sincere appraisal of the world. Yet it falls short of the gospel of Jesus Christ, which warns us repeatedly against making judgments only God can make. Nonetheless, these psalms remind us that a world lacking in transcendent accountability and in human responsibility, a world in which the oppressed cannot cry out in confidence for God's judgment against those who with impunity destroy and trample them, is a world that falls short of God's just reign. As painful as these psalms are to read—and as difficult as they may be to pray—they must not be forgotten or neglected if we are to reverence God's justice and respect human life.

# DAILY ASSIGNMENTS

This week we shall engage the psalms of wrath, listening for the vision of God's justice communicated through them. We will seek to understand why we resist praying these psalms and why we should not resist praying them. Finally, we will explore how these psalms can be heard in light of the gospel of Jesus Christ and how Christians may pray them.

Each day pray the psalm(s) for the day, read the accompanying biblical text(s), then pray the same psalm(s) again. The goal is to hear the psalms of wrath in the context of the biblical canon. After completing the assigned readings each day, consider the following questions:

- In what ways are the psalms of wrath consistent with the other assigned biblical texts?

- In what ways are the psalms of wrath in tension with the biblical texts?

- What sentiments in the psalms of wrath did you find most difficult to reconcile with the teachings of Jesus Christ?

**DAY ONE: Psalms 35; 36; 37; Exodus 13–15**

**DAY TWO: Psalms 5; 109; Isaiah 10–11**

**DAY THREE: Psalms 41; 58; 94; Hosea 6; Amos 7; Isaiah 42**

**DAY FOUR: Psalm 69; Luke 14; 17**

**DAY FIVE: Psalms 137; 139; Matthew 7; 11; 12**

**DAY SIX:**

Read the commentary in the participant book.

# THE WRATH OF GOD

To gain some perspective on the psalms of wrath, let's take a couple of steps back from the canvas on which the psalmist paints a portrait of human anger and outrage to see it in the larger context of an even greater wrath: the wrath of God.

According to the prophets of ancient Israel, God was angry at the repeated failure of humanity to live up to God's purposes for creation. The prophets warned the people of Israel of the scale of their failure, a failure that broke God's heart and led to God's own lamentations. We hear the Lord's lament in Isaiah's prophecy: "Hear, O heavens, and listen, O earth; / for the LORD has spoken: / I reared children and brought them up, / but they have rebelled against me. / The ox knows its owner, / and the donkey its master's crib; / but Israel does not know, / my people do not understand" (Isaiah 1:2-3).

God's lament, the expression of God's sorrow and unspeakable weariness with Israel, lay at the end of a road littered with human betrayal and divine disappointment. The people had observed religious niceties while spurning the love of God expressed in the Law. They were violent and unjust toward the poor and relatively powerless while ignoring God's call to mercy and justice. Isaiah tells us that the long-suffering kindness of God was treated with contempt by a people utterly absorbed in their own interests, hateful and divisive. They had forgotten their covenant role as children of God and varnished over their lust, violence, and self-aggrandizement with pious talk and cultic sacrifices.

Therefore, God's anger, as Isaiah tells us, "was kindled against his people" (Isaiah 5:25). "I cannot endure solemn assemblies with iniquity," the Lord says (Isaiah 1:13). The people's hypocrisy and arrogance were a misery to God, their idolatry an abomination. God's people had become a burden that the Lord was "weary of bearing" (Isaiah 1:14). In God's great sorrow, God acted in wrath. God used other nations to correct the people, to discipline them, in the hope that God could bring them back to themselves and to their Lord.

We have previously spoken of the tectonic tensions at work between the people's faith in the Lord who reigns and their experience of life's losses and pains. However, there is another tectonic rift running through the Old Testament between the faithfulness of God and the actions of an unfaithful humanity. God loves all creation (including humanity), and God creates all things in love. God graciously covenants with and recovers humanity repeatedly. Humanity repeatedly rejects God, rebels against God, and abandons God. The God whom the prophet describes in Isaiah 5:1 as "my beloved" watches in sorrow as the vineyard grows sour grapes instead of sweet ones. The vinedresser digs, clears, plants, waters, and protects the vineyard, only to suffer rejection. But running through these images of faithfulness is also the message of human faithlessness and of God's growing sorrow—and of God's growing wrath.

The wrath of God is "kindled" by the love of God. The love of God is not merely an abstract affection, the sort of ephemeral emotion we find illustrated on greeting cards. To say that God loves us is to say that God is freely and completely *for* us. God is not constrained to be for us. God is not compelled by anyone or by anything to create us. God is not forced to want the best for us, to seek us when we are lost, or to restore us when we fail. God loves us simply because of who God is: God is love. But the love of God is a consuming fire that burns away impurities. Any view of the love of God that does not understand the fierce, burning power of divine love—the positive force of God's love against sin, evil, and death—has resigned itself to mere sentimentalism, because the wrath of God is nothing less than the burning passion of God turned against all those things that threaten to destroy God's good creation.

The first step in understanding the psalms of wrath is to try to take justice and righteousness (and conversely to treat injustice and sin) as seriously as God does. When God turns against evil, and when God's wrath burns with consuming power against evil, it is because of what evil threatens to do to God's good creation. So to speak of the wrath of God is to speak of God's love turned against that which would destroy what God loves.

## The Cursing Psalms

A number of psalms cry out to God for vengeance, calling for God to destroy an enemy. These psalms are called imprecatory or cursing psalms (Psalms 35; 69; and 137, for example) and are sometimes avoided in Christian worship. German theologian Dietrich Bonhoeffer confirmed the importance of praying such psalms in spite of the difficult nature of their content: "I pray the imprecatory psalms in the certainty of their marvelous fulfillment. I leave the vengeance to God and ask him to execute his righteousness to all his enemies."[1]

# THE WRATH OF HUMANITY

The wrath of God should not be confused with human wrath, *even* when we are talking about the anger of religious people, *even* when our anger is fueled by righteous indignation, perhaps *especially* when we are seeking to know the heart and mind of God so that we can love what God loves and hate what God hates. The Psalms sometimes equate human wrath with God's wrath. "Contend, O LORD, with those who contend with me; / fight against those who fight against me! ... Let them be put to shame and dishonor / who seek after my life. / Let them be turned back and confounded / who devise evil against me. / Let them be like chaff before the wind, / with the angel of the LORD driving them on. / Let their way be dark and slippery, / with the angel of the LORD pursuing them" (Psalm 35:1, 4-6).

As we have seen, the wrath of God is nothing less than the love of God turned in fiery passion against that which would destroy God's creation and turned upon us to restore us to health and wholeness. But the wrath of humanity tends to serve the interests of base vindictiveness and revenge. Remembering that God's wrath should not be confused with our own, we can also recognize the fact that the human wrath reflected in these psalms (for all its obvious problems) expresses at least three important and positive spiritual impulses:

- There is nothing we experience or feel that should not be brought to God in prayer.

- There is an ultimate bar of divine justice before which we all shall stand.

- There is no doubt that we may have enemies; the real question is how we should treat them.

# BRINGING EVERYTHING TO GOD IN PRAYER

There is nothing we cannot and should not bring to God in prayer. This is the clear message of the psalms of wrath. The feeling that we have been slighted, the feeling that we have been sabotaged, the feeling that we have been used, abused, injured, or oppressed—all of these feelings and anything else can and should be brought to God in prayer. Our fury and indignation, our anger and smoldering resentments, even our ugliest feelings of self-righteousness and our lust for revenge—all can and should be brought to God in prayer. Without any filters that purify or self-censor the true nature of our feelings, we should speak our hearts and minds fully to God.

If we do *not* do this, we run the risk of hiding in the deepest and darkest recesses of our hearts the very things that most need to be seen in light of God's justice and mercy. Also, we run the risk of compartmentalizing our lives into a realm of piety and pretty sentiments under the banner of religion and another realm where we harbor hatred toward those people with whom we are in conflict. The psalms of wrath encourage us to bring everything we feel to God and to leave it there for God's judgment.

If we *are* willing to do this, we not only entrust to God the judgment we hope God will render on our behalf, but we also may learn to accept God's judgment when it differs from our own. We may even discover how to open ourselves to the searching light of God's judgment with respect to our own feelings of wrath and our desire for revenge. It is possible that when we pray, we may feel confirmed by God in our prayer. But it is also possible that as we rehearse in the presence of God our sense of having been wronged, we will see where we have also wronged others, and we will be drawn to pray for mercy, not only for ourselves but also for those who have wronged us. There is always a danger in prayer that we will be transformed, and not just someone else.

# THE BAR OF DIVINE JUSTICE

Whether standing beside a trench into which bodies of innocent villagers fall lifeless before a firing squad, or trudging along rows of a cotton field under the searing Delta sun, whether crowded into a sweltering jail cell in a prison camp, or living out exiled days far from a beloved homeland, genuine suffering does have a face. The psalmist knows this well. And those who experience suffering pray that someone somewhere is keeping score. The vengeance of God in the psalms of wrath is a searing expression of the hope that God keeps score, that God not only remembers our suffering (that God keeps our tears in a bottle, as Psalm 56:8 says), but that God holds accountable those who maliciously harm the innocent (that God will pour out his "indignation upon them" and that God's "burning anger" will "overtake them," as Psalm 69:24 says).

The psalms of wrath are furious psalms inspired by hope, specifically the hope that despots and tyrants who wreak havoc, oppression, and violence under the cover of darkness or under the cover of lies and secrecy cannot hide forever. One day they will be brought to justice. One day those who have suffered at their hands will be restored to health and wholeness. These psalms fervently believe that God is incorruptible, and before God's bar of justice everyone will stand, and justice will be rendered fairly.

Because God is just, because God's justice will not be circumvented or undermined, because God knows the whole story on all of us, and because only God is capable of rendering an appropriate judgment, judgment belongs only to God. The psalmist leaves judgment to God in the very passages where he cries out, "God of vengeance, shine forth! / Rise up, O judge of the earth" (Psalm 94:1b-2a). The psalmist is not above giving God some advice on what specific judgment God should render, but he does not take the accomplishment of retribution into his own hands. A superficial reading of the psalms of wrath often misses this fact, but the psalmist leaves the business of vengeance in God's hands.

# ENEMIES, A LOVE STORY

According to the Psalms, even God (who is holy and perfectly good) has enemies. For example, the psalms of wrath refer to those who love untruth, who are arrogant, who oppress the weak and persecute the righteous, who thirst for blood, and who slander their neighbors. According to the psalmist, these people are "enemies" of God. The psalmist sees the enemies of God as his own enemies, and he claims that he suffers at the hands of the evildoers because of his faithfulness to God.

There is real spiritual danger at this point. We have noted already how perilous it is both to our own souls and to the lives of others when we equate our ways with God's ways, and when we identify without distinction our enemies as God's. But there is a corresponding danger in not recognizing the duty to try to discern between good and evil, to try to identify with God's justice and mercy.

We can make enemies by doing good things, and sometimes we may be compelled to do so. A pastor who preceded me in a congregation I once served was threatened by the Ku-Klux-Klan because he and his family welcomed a black person into the worship of the church. The pastor made enemies—and they were real enemies. Another pastor I know began a ministry to the hungry and homeless persons in his congregation. While his congregation strongly supported the ministry, some civic leaders bitterly opposed it and for years worked hard to undermine the pastor's work. He made real enemies too.

It is possible for Christians to have enemies. Indeed, sometimes our true character is known as much by the quality of our enemies as by the quality of our friends. The question is, how does a Christian respond to enemies? We cannot afford to let go of the claim that God makes on us for the sake of justice; nor can we abandon God's claim on us for the sake of mercy. We may have enemies, and we may hate what they do. But we cannot hate them, nor can we treat them with disrespect. Indeed, we are called by Jesus Christ to love them and to pray for them because they also are loved by God.

The psalms of wrath may represent a first step in an appropriate response to our enemies: They require us to recognize their existence. But while we should acknowledge them when we pray, we must also recognize that, according to Jesus Christ, our treatment of our enemies is as essential to our Christian witness as our own attempts to do justice and to live righteously. Indeed, repeatedly we are told that God's forgiveness of us depends on our forgiveness of those who sin against us (Matthew 6:14-15; Mark 11:25-26; Luke 6:35-37). As followers of Christ we are called to treat our enemies as Christ treated his enemies: "Father, forgive them; for they do not know what they are doing" (Luke 23:34).

### The Bay Psalm Book

The first book to be completely written and printed in the American colonies was a collection of psalms to be sung in worship entitled The Bay Psalm Book: The Whole Booke of Psalmes Faithfully Translated Into English Meter. Published in 1640, this versification in English of all 150 psalms contained text only but included directions for locating appropriate tunes in another Psalter.

So we continue to pray the psalms of wrath, but without self-righteous satisfaction and without the intent to destroy those with whom we are in conflict. We continue to pray, but always as Christians, praying these psalms *through* our Lord Jesus Christ. And when we do, we must also be prepared to know our enemies anew and to love them.

# INVITATION TO DISCIPLESHIP

For many Christians, the psalms of wrath are very hard to hear. While the good news of Jesus Christ recognizes the disturbing fact that we will have enemies, it is clear in its instructions regarding how we are to deal with them. We know we are to love our enemies, not pray God's judgment on their heads. But we less frequently realize the connection between Christ's command to love our enemies and the claim of the kingdom of God—or as the Psalms express it, the reign of the Lord—upon our lives. The reason we are called to love our enemies is because the Lord reigns over us and over them. We all belong to the Lord, and we bear witness to the character of the Lord to whom we belong precisely by loving our enemies—even when we feel vengeful toward them.

Some have suggested that Jesus' teachings in the Sermon on the Mount are intended to set the bar impossibly high so that we are driven to seek God's grace. Certainly Jesus' call is demanding and his discipleship costly, and God's grace in all of life is our only hope. But surely Jesus did not preach the whole Sermon on the Mount with his tongue in his cheek. No, Jesus calls us beyond the wrath of humankind to the love that is the essence of God's character, the love that forgives the inexcusable, that inspires the penitent to change, that shames the guilty and offers us a way out of the cycle of vengeance and violence that grips our world.

# FOR REFLECTION

- The wrath of God is a contentious subject. Some Christians would prefer to believe that God is never wrathful, that God's love is pure affirmation. However, the Psalms reflect a belief that God's wrath represents a burning zeal in God to destroy that which would destroy God's good creation. From the perspective of the Psalms, what is lost if God is only a God of love and not also a God of wrath?

- The commentary explores briefly the danger of equating God's wrath with human wrath. What are the dangers you see in confusing our anger with God's?

- The enemies of which the Psalms speak are ordinarily human adversaries seeking to ridicule, harm, or kill the psalmist. If you placed yourself in the shoes of the psalmist, from whom would you seek relief? What enemies do you have that are not human adversaries? Temptations? Aspects of our culture? Possessions? Objects of false worship? How do you bring them to God in prayer?

- When you come across psalms calling for action you find objectionable or repulsive, how have you dealt with them? The Psalms encourage us to bring everything to God in prayer. When have you felt hesitant to bring problems or emotions, including anger or wrath, to God in prayer? What might it mean for you to ask Christ to pray these psalms for you?

## According to the Psalms, God is...

Shield (Psalm 3:3)
King (Psalm 10:16)
Rock (Psalm 18:2)
Redeemer (Psalm 19:14)
Shepherd (Psalm 23:1)
Light (Psalm 27:1)
Helper (Psalm 54:4)
Refuge (Psalm 62:8)
Hope (Psalm 71:5)
Portion (Psalm 73:26)
Maker (Psalm 95:6)
Keeper (Psalm 121:5)

# Hallelujah and Amen

*Praise the LORD! / How good it is to sing praises to our God; / for he is gracious, and a song of praise is fitting. . . . Sing to the LORD with thanksgiving; / make melody to our God on the lyre.*

—*Psalm 147:1, 7*

## INTRODUCTION

The title of the Book of Psalms in the Hebrew Bible could be translated into English as "Praises" or "The Book of Praises." At the most basic level, the Psalms are simply this: The praises of the people of Israel to the Lord their God. We have seen, however, that the praises of Israel are often grounded in harrowing experiences of social disruption, political oppression, religious upheaval, and personal distress; and these experiences are sometimes reflected in psalms of lament and wrath. The psalmists cry out for deliverance in all sorts of crises. The praises of Israel do not exist in isolation from the historical and social tensions in which the nation negotiated its faith or the personal stresses in which a particular psalmist tried to understand his relationship with God. The praise voiced in the Psalms is a "knowing" praise, not superficial praise. It is grounded in an abiding awareness of the human condition. The psalmists are conscious of the backdrop of suffering against which they praise and give thanks to God.

The psalmists are also conscious of the change of heart and mind that may be required in order for us to praise God. Imagine: We begin a prayer blaming God for the things we have suffered, yet we discover in light of more mature reflection that after all, God is not to blame—we are. Or imagine we begin a prayer demanding that God take up our cause, only to discover in prayer that our cause is unrighteous and untenable. Perhaps we begin a prayer asking God to visit retribution on our enemies, assuming that our enemies are also God's enemies, but realize as we pray that what is required is not revenge but forgiveness. In any of these circumstances, we may—in the act of praying—learn to praise God from a new vantage point, having gained a new perspective on who God is and who we are.

# DAILY ASSIGNMENTS

This week we shall pray some of the most beautiful psalms ever written. These psalms employ the full register of the psalmist's eloquence to communicate a consciousness of the presence of an infinitely adorable God. Pray the psalm(s) for each day as your own expression of praise to God. Read the other biblical texts, listening for the ways in which the early church glorified God in their worship.

## DAY ONE: Psalms 124; 129; Luke 1:46-55; 2:29-32

These two psalms declare God's praise in response to God's deliverance. After praying these psalms, read the songs of Mary and Simeon. You read them earlier in Session 2, but what do you hear now in these New Testament psalms you did not hear before?

## DAY TWO: Psalms 107; 136; Romans 5; 11:33-36

Biblical scholars categorize these two praise psalms as "descriptive" psalms of praise. After praying them, pray Paul's doxology in Romans 11:33-36. How does praying this passage from Romans instead of simply reading it affect the way you hear it? Then read Romans 5, in which Paul explores in prose the grace of God. The Old Testament psalms of praise and the doxologies of the New Testament both respond to the character of the God revealed. Reflect on these passages from the Psalms and Romans, particularly the various dimensions of God's grace described and celebrated in all these biblical texts. What does grace (kindness, mercy) look like in the Psalms?

## DAY THREE: Psalms 100; 117; Romans 16:25-27; Ephesians 3:14-21

For many Protestants, Psalm 100 and the Doxology (the hymn "Praise God From Whom All Blessings Flow" sung in worship after the offerings of the people) are closely linked. Pray the texts of Psalm 100 and the Doxology. The New Testament doxologies for this week truly are doxologies in the fullest sense of the term: ascriptions of praise to God. What exactly do these doxologies praise God for?

## DAY FOUR: Psalms 147; 148; Colossians 1:15-20; Revelation 4:8-11

It is not surprising that Psalms 147 and 148 have entered the hymnody of the church. However, what may be surprising is that the passage from Colossians, which is usually translated as prose, may in fact have been a hymn (or derived from a hymn) of the early church. The text from Revelation is the basis for several great hymns: "Holy, Holy, Holy! Lord God Almighty"; "Let All Mortal Flesh Keep Silence"; and "Hail, Thou Once Despised Jesus."

After praying the psalms and the biblical doxologies for the day, choose one of these hymns to sing.

## DAY FIVE: Psalms 149; 150; Revelation 7:12, 15-17; 11:15-18; 21:3-4

These texts from the Psalms and from the Book of Revelation look forward into God's promised future. A people who have known suffering, exile, and oppression are invited to sing "a new song"; they are invited to "sing for joy on their couches" (Psalm 149:1, 5). The hymns "Praise the Lord Who Reigns Above" and "Praise to the Lord, the Almighty" are both based on Psalm 150. Charles Wesley's "Ye Servants of God" is based on Revelation 7:9-12; and the African American spiritual "I Want to Be Ready" reflects themes from Revelation 21. Pray the psalms and the doxologies from Revelation. Then choose one of these hymns to pray or sing.

## DAY SIX:

Read the commentary in the participant book.

# PRAISE DECLARED, PRAISE DESCRIBED

Scholars today tend to place the psalms of praise into two categories: *declarative* psalms and *descriptive* psalms. According to scholar W. H. Bellinger, the declarative psalms of praise provide "the link between lament and praise." He calls them "psalms of thanksgiving because they offer praise and thanks to God based on the deliverance the psalm narrates." And he contrasts these psalms with the descriptive psalm of praise, "which describes God as praiseworthy in more general terms: God as creator, sovereign, nurturer."[1]

Bellinger's distinction between the psalms of thanksgiving (declarative psalms of praise) and what many call the hymns of praise (descriptive psalms of praise) clarifies these types of praise psalms in a helpful manner. In this context, psalms of thanksgiving express our gratitude for what God has done. Hymns of praise express our adoration of God, our praise of God, for who God is. According to Bellinger, there are eight individual psalms of thanksgiving: Psalms 30; 34; 41; 66; 92; 116; 118; and 138; and there are six community psalms of thanksgiving: Psalms 67; 75; 107; 124; 129; and 136.[2]

Listen for a moment to the way Psalm 124 (a community psalm of thanksgiving) frames the praise of God as thanksgiving: "If it had not been the LORD who was on our side / —let Israel now say— / if it had not been the LORD who was on our side, / when our enemies attacked us, / then they would have swallowed us up alive.... Blessed be the LORD, / who has not given us / as prey to their teeth.... Our help is in the name of the LORD, / who made heaven and earth" (124:1-3a, 6, 8).

## Selah

"Prayer is fundamentally liturgical. *Selah*, untranslated and untranslatable, strewn through the Psalms, will not let us forget it. If its *meaning* is an enigma, its *use* is clear: *Selah* directed people who were *together* in prayer to do something or other *together*.... Biblically, we are not provided with a single prayer for private devotions. The community in prayer, not the individual at prayer, is basic and primary."[3]

*(Eugene H. Peterson)*

The structure of Psalm 34 (an individual psalm of thanksgiving) is different from 124, but the spirit of gratitude for what God has done is essentially the same. It begins with praise: "I will bless the LORD at all times; / his praise shall continually be in my mouth. / My soul makes its boast in the LORD; / let the humble hear and be glad. / O magnify the LORD with me, / and let us exalt his name together." Why? Because "I sought the LORD, and he answered me, / and delivered me from all my fears" (34:1-4).

Rather than responding directly to God's deliverance from a dangerous situation or a lamentable circumstance, the hymns of praise describe through the language of praise God's reign, eternal majesty, creative power, faithfulness, and loving kindness—in other words, God's character. Listen for the quality of praise offered in some of these psalms. For example, Psalm 29: "Ascribe to the LORD, O heavenly beings, / ascribe to the LORD glory and strength. / Ascribe to the LORD the glory of his name; / worship the LORD in holy splendor" (29:1-2). Here the psalmist is praising God for who God is. The psalmist is praising God not simply because God has answered a specific prayer or rescued him from a distressing situation, but because God is holy, righteous, faithful, steadfast, and good. The hymns of praise might also be called prayers of adoration, a kind of prayer less common in Christian worship today than prayers of confession (in which we pray for forgiveness), petition (in which we ask God for something), and intercession (in which we offer up to God the needs of others).

# LEARNING TO SAY
# HALLELUJAH, AMEN

In popular Christian culture, when someone says, "Praise the Lord!" it often means little more than "That's great!" "I'm glad this happened!" or "Hurray for our side!" It has become a virtually empty phrase on the lips of many, uttered at the drop of a hat. Sometimes it might even lapse into the category of taking the Lord's name in vain.

For the Psalms, by contrast, to say, "Praise the Lord," is to thank God for God's deliverance of us. To say, "Praise the Lord," is to adore God for God's character. In the Psalms, "praise the Lord" is never just a shout of victory or elation. Sometimes "hallelujah" expresses the culmination of a struggle of the soul in which the person of faith has lived through the shifts and terrors of life, has witnessed the deep movements of God in the world, and has emerged with "amen" on his or her lips, finally able to say with relief or hard-won conviction, "So be it, Lord!" When the psalmist praises the Lord, he is not so much lifted up in a hyper-emotional state as he is brought down to earth in the realization that he stands on hallowed ground. If the psalms of penitence turn us around and set us off in a new direction, the psalms of praise map out that direction for us. They make clear the purposes and ends for which God created us.

# TO ENJOY GOD FOREVER

"It is right to give our thanks and praise." We say this each time we celebrate the Lord's Supper. Why is it right to give God our thanks and praise? Not just because gratitude is the proper response of beings who depend upon the creative power of God for their very existence. Not just because praise is the only really sane response from a human creature who has become conscious of the unutterable greatness, wonder, beauty, love, and delight of God. And not just because thanks and praise are duties we owe God for the reality of being. Why is it right to give God our thanks and praise? Because we were made to live thankfully, joyfully, and in an attitude of praise. Because a spirit of gratitude and praise is the fuel on which a spiritually healthy humanity runs.

The psalms of praise reflect the fullness of human life for which we were created. They inhale the creative life of God and exhale gratitude and praise. They do what is natural. They remind us that to withhold praise and thanksgiving from God is as unnatural as trying to run a marathon while holding our breath.

For example, Psalm 136 conveys the rhythms of a runner inhaling the goodness of God and exhaling praise:

> *O give thanks to the* LORD, *for he is good,*
> *for his steadfast love endures forever.*
> *O give thanks to the God of gods,*
> *for his steadfast love endures forever.*
> *O give thanks to the Lord of lords,*
> *for his steadfast love endures forever;*
> *who alone does great wonders,*
> *for his steadfast love endures forever. (Psalm 136:1-4)*

Notice throughout the rest of the psalm how the psalmist races through Creation and Exodus and the occupation of the Promised Land, from beside the streams of Exile to the courts of the new Temple, from remembrances of God's deliverance in times of danger to the simple daily provision of food in the wilderness, inhaling the loving kindness of God (*hesed*, in Hebrew) and exhaling praise (*hallelujah*). One can imagine a congregation racing through this litany of praise, then sitting down abruptly afterward, dizzy from too much oxygen acquired too fast. A congregation reciting this psalm of praise at the right pace would end up as winded as an Easter choir at the end of Handel's "Hallelujah" chorus. We praise God in the psalms of praise and we sing hallelujah because, as Handel himself reminds us, "He shall reign forever and ever. King of kings and Lord of lords. Hallelujah! Hallelujah!"[4]

Praising God is the natural and necessary response of the faithful to the reign of the Lord. The Psalms themselves ground this praise in God's deliverance of his people from slavery and in God's restoration of his people from exile. The Psalms ground their praise in a dumbfounded, flatfooted wonder in the presence of a God who is good and gracious beyond all imaginings.

When Mary sings of the reign of God scattering the proud, bringing down the powerful from their thrones, filling the hungry with good things, and sending the rich away empty (Luke 1:51-53), the right response is to praise God. And when an angel tells the shepherds, "To you is born this day in the city of David a Savior, who is the Messiah, the Lord," the right response is to sing, "Glory to God in the highest heaven, / and on earth peace among those whom he favors!" (Luke 2:11, 14).

When John the Baptist preaches, "The one who is more powerful than I is coming after me; I am not worthy to stoop down and untie the thong of his sandals. I have baptized you with water; but he will baptize you with the Holy Spirit" (Mark 1:7-8), the right response is to exclaim, "Praise God!"

When Jesus is in the synagogue in Nazareth and reads the prophet Isaiah, "The Spirit of the Lord is upon me, / because he has anointed me / to bring good news to the poor. / He has sent me to proclaim release to the captives / and recovery of sight to the blind, / to let the oppressed go free, / to proclaim the year of the Lord's favor," and when Jesus rolls up the scroll, sits down, and says, "Today this scripture has been fulfilled in your hearing" (Luke 4:18-21), the right response of the congregation is to proclaim, "Hallelujah!"

And when we are told that the kingdom of God is among us and in us, that the poor, the merciful, the pure of heart, and the peacemakers are blessed, that any who want to become followers of Jesus must deny themselves, take up their cross, and follow him, the right response is to declare, "So be it! Amen."

# INVITATION TO DISCIPLESHIP

We were created in the image of God. This is a founding principle of our faith. The temptation, of course, is to turn this principle around, to try to create a God in our image. The temptation is to make a God as small as we are, a God who represents our interests and perspectives, a God who could never imagine possibilities that we cannot admit, a God who exists only to serve us.

The Psalms resist this temptation at every turn, especially when they teach us to make our lives into living hallelujahs and amens spoken to the God who reigns. Because the Psalms recognize that we were created to praise God, they invite us to praise and love God for who God is rather than to love the little images of God we have made in our own likeness. The Psalms call us to enjoy God and glorify God for what God does rather than to try to reduce God to our narrow concerns. The Psalms challenge us to see the world through eyes enlarged by eternity and to see all that makes this world holy, mysterious, and wonderful, because it belongs to God.

When the Psalms invite us to praise the Lord and to say amen to God's mighty acts in history, they are lobbying us to allow our hearts to be transformed so that we will share the character of the God we worship. To say amen to the reign of the Lord opens a portal into the impossible possibility of God in our midst. One may conclude, at last, that when hallelujah is finally pulled from our mortal souls, it will mean far more than the trite formula of popular piety. Rather, it will represent a whole life repentant, restored, amazed in the presence of God, as we recognize a purpose more gracious, just and good than we ever imagined possible, and we cry out in utter surprise, "So this is what you were doing all along! Hallelujah! Amen!"

# FOR REFLECTION

- The Psalms express faith in a God who is purposeful, a God who is personally involved in creation and history and works towards redemptive ends. How would you compare the understanding of God expressed in the Psalms to the God revealed in Jesus Christ and proclaimed in the early church? How would you compare the understanding of God expressed in the Psalms to contemporary understandings of God represented by your own church or by the culture at large?

- The holiness of God is a theme that runs through the Psalms no less than the immediacy of God. Where in your experience of worship is the holiness of God most honored? Where is the immediacy or intimacy of God most evident? What do you think is important about beginning worship with praise?

- The words *hallelujah* and *amen* are invested with great significance in the Psalms. What would it mean to invest the words with equal significance in our Christian lives? What would it mean to articulate God's praise in such a way that it carries the full force of an hallelujah? What would it mean to speak the word *amen* in such a way that it says in all of life, "So be it, Lord"?

- Having lived in the midst of the Psalms for some weeks now, what new insights have you gained? How have the Psalms challenged or deepened your practice of faith? What aspects of God's character have you glimpsed anew in the Psalms?

## Psalm 151

According to the tables of contents of
the TANAKH (Hebrew Bible) and
Christian Bibles today, the Book of Psalms
contains only 150 psalms. Scholars, however,
have long known of the existence of additional
psalms. For example, the Greek translation of the
Hebrew Bible—the Septuagint (LXX)—included
Psalm 151. A Hebrew language version of Psalm
151 (with some variations) was also found on a
Psalm scroll discovered at Qumran, dating from
30–50 AD. The New Revised Standard
Version (NRSV) Bible includes Psalm
151 as part of its Apocryphal/
Deuterocanonical
Books section.

# ENDNOTES

## INTRODUCTION

1. From *Commentary on the Book of Psalms*, by John Calvin, translated by the Rev. James Anderson (Baker Book House, 1984); page xxxvii.

## SESSION 1

1. From *Prayerbook of the Bible: An Introduction to the Psalms*, by Dietrich Bonhoeffer, in Dietrich Bonhoeffer Works, Vol. 5, translated by James H. Burtness (Fortress Press, 1996).

2. From *Prayerbook of the Bible*; page 156.

3. From "Preface to the Psalter," in *Works of Martin Luther*, Vol. VI (Muhlenberg Press, 1932); page 385.

4. From *The New Interpreter's Bible*, Vol. IV, commentary on the Book of Psalms, by J. Clinton McCann, Jr. (Abingdon Press, 1996); pages 642–43.

5. From *The Psalms Through Three Thousand Years: Prayerbook of a Cloud of Witnesses*, by William L. Holladay (Fortress Press, 1993); page 115.

6. From *Prayerbook of the Bible*; page 157.

7. From *Commentary on the Book of Psalms*, by John Calvin, translated by the Rev. James Anderson (Baker Book House, 1984); page xxxvii.

## SESSION 2

1. From *Answering God: The Psalms as Tools for Prayer*, by Eugene H. Peterson (HarperSanFrancisco, 1989); page 5.

2. From *Wondrous Depth: Preaching the Old Testament*, by Ellen F. Davis (Westminster John Knox Press, 2005); page 21.

3. There are a number of accessible general articles on the Psalms that provide a summary of current scholarship. I have found the following particularly helpful in writing these introductory paragraphs: *The New Westminster Dictionary of the Bible*, edited by Henry Snyder Gehman (The Westminster Press, 1970); pages 772–75; *The Interpreter's Dictionary of the Bible*, Vol. III, edited by George Arthur Buttrick (Abingdon Press, 1962); pages 942–58; *Handbook to the Old Testament*, by Claus Westermann (Augsburg Publishing House, 1976); pages 210–25;

"The Book of Psalms," in *The New Interpreter's Bible*, Vol. IV, by J. Clinton McCann, Jr. (Abingdon Press, 1996); pages 641–77; and *The Old Testament: A Historical and Literary Introduction to the Hebrew Scriptures*, by Michael D. Coogan (Oxford University Press, 2006); pages 456–68.

4. See *Christian Hymns Observed: When in Our Music God Is Glorified*, by Erik Routley (Prestige Publications, Inc., 1982); pages 15–22.


## SESSION 3

1. From *Saint Benedict's Rule*, translated by Patrick Barry OSB (Ampleforth Abbey Press, 1997); page 99.

2. See *I and Thou*, by Martin Buber, translated by Walter Kaufmann (Charles Scribner's Sons, 1970); page 62.

3. From "Confessions: Book Nine," in *Augustine: Confessions and Enchiridion*, Vol. VII, translated and edited by Albert C. Outler (The Westminster Press, 1955); page 183.


## SESSION 4

1. See *The Living Psalms*, by Claus Westermann, translated by J. R. Porter (T. & T. Clark Ltd., 1989); pages 18–19.

2. From *Seeing the Psalms: A Theology of Metaphor*, by William P. Brown (Westminster John Knox Press, 2002); page 214.

3. From *Given: Poems*, by Wendell Berry. Copyright 2006 by Wendell Berry. Reprinted by permission of the publisher.

4. Excerpt from "The Rain Stick," from *Opened Ground: Selected Poems 1966–1996*, by Seamus Heaney. Copyright © 1998 by Seamus Heaney. Reprinted by permission of Farrar, Straus and Giroux, LLC.

5. From "Introduction to Poetry," in *Sailing Alone Around the Room*, by Billy Collins (Random House, 2001); page 16.


## SESSION 5

1. Quoted from St. Ambrose (c. 339–397), in *The Biblical Psalms in Christian Worship: A Brief Introduction and Guide to Resources*, by John D. Witvliet (William B. Eerdmans Publishing Company, 2007); pages 4–5.

## SESSION 6

1. The phrase *language world* is from "With These Words: The Language World of the Psalms," in *The Lord Reigns: A Theological Handbook to the Psalms*, by James L. Mays (Westminster John Knox Press, 1994); pages 3–11.

2. See Gunkel's major and minor types of psalms as described in *The Testimony of Poets and Sages: The Psalms and Wisdom Literature*, by W. H. Bellinger, Jr. (Smyth & Helwys Publishing, Inc., 1998); pages 10–11. See additional types of psalms mentioned in the index of *Out of the Depths: The Psalms Speak for Us Today*, by Bernhard W. Anderson (The Westminster Press, 1983).

3. From *The Lord Reigns*; page 7.

4. From *Reflections on the Psalms*, by C. S. Lewis (Harcourt Brace Jovanovich, Publishers, 1958); page 97.

## SESSION 7

1. From *The Souls of Black Folk*, by W. E. B. Du Bois (Penguin Books, 1989); pages 207–08.

2. See the section on musical instruments in *The Interpreter's Dictionary of the Bible: An Illustrated Encyclopedia*, Vol. K–Q (Abingdon Press, 1962); pages 469–76.

3. Walter Brueggemann explores this movement from orientation to new orientation in *Praying the Psalms* (St. Mary's Press, 1982) and at greater length in *The Message of the Psalms* (Augsburg, 1984).

4. From *Praying the Psalms*; page 7.

## SESSION 8

1. Prayers from the Penitential Service are taken from the Book of Common Prayer (Oxford University Press); pages 72, 264–69.

2. From *The Cloister Walk*, by Kathleen Norris (Riverhead Books, 1996); page 100.

3. From the Book of Common Prayer; pages 41–42.

4. From *The Psalms and Their Meaning for Today*, by Samuel Terrien (The Bobbs-Merrill Company, Inc., 1952); pages 170–71.

5. From *The Psalms and Their Meaning for Today*; page 171.

6. See *Worship, Community, and the Triune God of Grace*, by James B. Torrance (Paternoster Press, 1996); page 44.

7. From *The Psalms and Their Meaning for Today*; page 171.


**SESSION 9**

1. From *Psalms: The Prayer Book of the Bible*, by Dietrich Bonhoeffer, translated by James H. Burtness (Augsburg Publishing House, 1970); page 59.


**SESSION 10**

1. From *Psalms: Reading and Studying the Book of Praises*, by W. H. Bellinger, Jr. (Hendrickson Publishers, 1990); page 75.

2. From *Psalms*; page 75.

3. From *Answering God: The Psalms as Tools for Prayer*, by Eugene H. Peterson (HarperSanFrancisco, 1989); pages 83–84.

4. From Handel's *Messiah*, by George Frederick Handel.